DYNAMIC

DYNAMIC

A CHRISTIAN FAITH

ENOCH HANG

Second Edition

Copyright © 2020 by Enoch Hang. All rights reserved.

The events and conversations in this book have been set down to the author's best ability. All quotes by individuals are best attempts at paraphrasing.

Printed in the United States of America.

ISBN: 978-1-7341880-0-4

Illustrations © 2019 by Taysha Kim, Mikaya Kim, Samuel Sunito, Shannon Jiang, Theresa Li, Emily Lu, Breanna De Vera, Jasper Leong , Shoshana Tai, and Catherine Wu.
Designed by Hannah Hiler
The text of this book was set in Lora

CONTENTS

0: Preface 1

1: Dynamic 5

2: The Moving Spirit of God 13

3: Perfect, Not Balanced 23

4: Freedom in Structure 35

5: Dynamic Spiritual Disciplines 45

6: God's Plan 57

7: Complete Images of God 69

8: Revival 85

9: Faith, a Reflex 91

10: Love 103

11: Moment by Moment 119

Final Chapter: Static 125

CHAPTER 0:

Preface

DYNAMIC

Dynamic is a word that when used, implies one of the highest orders of positive connotations to its subject. It often subconsciously tears down the limits that one has placed on the subject of conversation. I apply this subtle concept to God within the Christian faith in hopes of breaking down the limits that people have placed on God subconsciously.

Main Idea:

Dynamic is alive. When we ask about who God is we need to ask if what we're defining or confining Him to is dynamic or static. If we define Him with something static, we might find ourselves exploring a dead god.

DYNAMIC: A CHRISTIAN FAITH

BELOVED,

By the infinite grace of God, the perfect love of our Lord
Jesus, and the fellowship of His Holy Spirit in faith I am writing
to you.[1]

DISCLAIMERS

I had no desire to write this book at all. I thought to myself
"if I were to write a book on this topic what if I ironically made
this word static." Even as I do so now, I am reluctant to write this.
But I come by the invitation of those whom I have already shared
this good news and life. The Holy Spirit has also spurred me into
exploring Him in His fullness through this. I obediently bring
myself here with a mustard seed of excitement and faith. All glory
be to God, not me, please.

As I am writing this, I am only 22[2] years of age. I have no
reason to believe that I am more wise, more knowledgeable, or
more discerning than those more advanced in their years with our
Lord Jesus. But what I do believe is that there is always room for a
fresh breath of God's Word to enter anyone's life at any time.

This is by no means a way of implying that I have all
authority and wisdom, so take this with a grain of salt, a light
heart, and a seat of a new perspective. And for those who do not

---

[1] Who do I sound like? (Haha)

[2] I had wished this book to be finished within a few months. But now 23,
I'm still finding a few new things to include.

— 2 —

0: PREFACE

consider themselves Christian, include also a hint of skepticism and humility as you take on this book.

The entire narrative is not written in the pursuit of becoming a theological or intellectual work, but rather a collection of experiences and thought processes.

The goal is not to create a new religion of some sorts or to add to the Word of God or take away from it, but rather to help us see Him with new eyes for who He is or at least restart the dialogue of it. I hope to take you through the journey that God has taken me through in this life so far. I invite you to revisit with me the events that have occurred, the thoughts that have gone through my mind, and the emotions and wrestling that I have faced with Him.

BOOK STRUCTURE

Within this book, I have written with a structure that can be freely read with the first chapter first and the last chapter last. Obviously. But, the rest of the chapters are standalone within those two chapters, so go ahead and adventure through these chapters in any order you would like.[3] Together, the chapters will still be coherent and comprehensible when brought together with the first and final chapter.[4] The goal is to bring you the heart that has been given me about the Gospel and of God. **What you**

---

[3] The chapters were written in this order: 1, 2, 4, 3, 5, 8, 11, 6, 9, 7, 10, 12

[4] Headings and subtitles are important!

read here I hope you do not take word for word, but would instead experience my heart, hopefully the heart God has given me.

CHAPTER 1:

DYNAMIC

DYNAMIC STORY

This is the most important part of the book, so pay close attention. Here I start the story and basis in which I write the rest of this book, with the word dynamic. What's the first thing that comes to your mind when you see or hear that word used?

- *"That was a **dynamic** speaker."*
- *"That team was very **dynamic**."*
- *"The **dynamic** of the company fits me perfectly."*
- *Dynamics (Physics)*
- *Musical Dynamics*

Let me take you through what goes on through my head when I hear this word.

DYNAMIC ORIGINS

At the end of my first year at the University of Southern California (USC)[5], I was invited to play a game called "Top Five Loves" by a friend, Faith,[6] with a group of others at a conference hosted by InterVarsity, a parachurch geared towards college students. This game was meant to help explore some of our deepest desires and pleasures along with the intention of stepping into deeper friendships with one another, like late night talks. The instructions: to label what the top five things in this world that you loved the most besides God, family, friends and why.

While Faith was sharing hers as an example, in my mind I immediately labeled ice cream, nature, and the word dynamic and proceeded to share these following hers. It is understandable to my fellow ice cream fiends reading that ice cream was at the top of my incomplete list. There's nothing as refreshing, as sweet, and as elegant as an ice cold, creamy treat[7] any day. For my nature-loving readers, the ecosystems, natural adaptability, and intricate systems of life that interacts with you when basking in its presence gives this energy and connection unlike anything else.

Finally, the word *dynamic*. I was surprised myself, not knowing exactly why but felt compelled to say. Deep within me I knew that it didn't just come out of nowhere. My first reason included that I loved the way that the word was used, for example

---

[5] The year 2016 "FIGHT ON!"

[6] Faith Victoria Wang, a fellow sister in Christ that I had met that year.

[7] Mind you, I'm also lactose intolerant.

1: DYNAMIC

like "dynamic speaker" or "dynamic of a team", they all added this meaning to its subject that meant more than just adaptability, power, or capability.

Another key example for me was "dynamic memory allocation," a term that as a computer science major I grew to know so well. Basically, when you decide to run your computer program, usually, the "computer" requires that you tell it exactly how much memory you plan on using through concrete numbers (1, 2, 3, etc.). Though sometimes even you don't know how much memory you'll need at the time you start the program. So, the "computer" allows us to instead of statically "creating" memory with concrete numbers in the beginning, decide how much memory we need whenever we want within our program with a chosen variable (x, y, z, etc.). So depending on the specific time and situation, the correct amount of memory will be allocated![8]

By the end of this game, everyone thought I was too obscure and mocked me for choosing this word, but it was okay! Even I did not truly understand what I meant, and I'm sure the same goes for you right now. But this marked the beginning of my journey to finding the fullness of this word.

Since then and even before, being involved with my faith and relationship with God, I found myself in a constant struggle with the very minute inconsistencies between the God that the Church around was showing me versus the God that I was experiencing for myself. Not only was I finding it hard to reconcile with the God

---

[8] I apologize to my fellow computer science experts; I am oversimplifying the subject.

DYNAMIC: A CHRISTIAN FAITH

they were showing me, but it also challenged the structures and ideologies that I have grown to know so well.

More specifically, this included:

- Inviting friends of mine that were Christian or non-christian to my church where I myself was uncomfortable with the structure and way things were done.
- God is one who provides free will vs. God is one who has predestined everything.
- The lives of most of the Christians I knew lived like functional Atheists.
- God's justice and love includes genocide in the Old Testament.
- Not seeing many non-believers choose to follow Jesus but even for those who did, seeing them turn away from him.
- God's justice and grace only allows for some people to be with Him in eternity.
- The tragedies that were happening all around the world yet God is sovereign and all-powerful.
- God's love should be so desirable and accepted yet many people leave the church.
- Good news isn't so good to many of the people that hear it, especially the poor or alien.
- Churches choose to discriminate against certain people even within a faith where we are called to love everyone.
- Living in the victory of Christ as a new creation but forfeiting to my earthly desires easily.
- and much more!

Despite it all, I still spent almost every morning with God in devotion to Him. Some days I found myself writing into my journal

— 8 —

so passionately some heart-filled profound understandings of who He was. They were always a result of me desperately wrestling with God about these irreconcilable ideas of who He was within me.

I would sit there trying to fathom what I had just wrote and cross reference it with the Bible to see if it made sense at all. I would then go around sharing it with my brothers and sisters, mentors, and disciplers of faith with excitement hoping that they would call me out for heresy, but each time I was met with excitement and joy in faith. Each time these revelations came, I found them leading back to some aspects of what I now know the word **dynamic** to be.

But what does the word *dynamic* actually mean? What is its definition? Where does it come from? After doing some research on the internet and referencing a few dictionaries I put together what I found in the following:

DYNAMIC

adjective
1. *characterized as constant change, activity or process*
2. *positive in attitude and full of energy and new ideas*
3. *relating to forces producing motion (physics)*
4. *denoting or relating to web pages that update frequently or are generated according to an individual's search terms (programming)*
5. *affected by the passage of time or the presence/ absence of power*

DYNAMIC: A CHRISTIAN FAITH

noun

1. *a force that stimulates change or progress within a system or process*

Webster: *marked by usually continuous and productive activity or change*

root word >> *dunamis (Greek - δύναμις, εως, ἡ) >> physical power, force, might, ability, efficacy, energy, meaning*

What does this have to do with anything God-related?

Recently, a good friend of mine, Mike Parkyn, and I had been talking quite frequently. I mentioned to him in one of our conversations that I wanted to describe God as **dynamic**, every part of the word. I asked if it was biblical to describe Him as one that was in constant change, activity or progress, full of power, might, energy, and meaning. He took me to Acts 1:8 in the Bible.

In Acts, the second book by Luke, the story starts post-Jesus' death and resurrection, right before His ascension. His disciples, following Him to the mount called Olivet, ask Him about the restoration of the kingdom of Israel and when that was to happen. Jesus responds,

> "It is not for you to know times or seasons that the Father has fixed by his own authority. But you will receive power when the Holy Spirit has come upon you, and you will be my

1: DYNAMIC

witnesses in Jerusalem and in all Judea and Samaria, and to the end of the earth." (Acts 1:7-8 ESV)

Mike pointed me to the word "power" and took me to the interlinear version of it, the original greek word "dunamis". WOW. SPEECHLESS. This is the same word used to derive the word dynamic![9] I re-read that sentence over again but now using *dynamic* to help give me a better sense of "dunamis" and WOW.

*"It is not for you to know times or seasons that the Father has fixed by his own authority. But you will receive **dynamic** when the Holy Spirit has come upon you, and you will be my witnesses in Jerusalem and in all Judea and Samaria, and to the end of the earth."*
(Acts 1:7-8 ESV - Enoch edit)

SPEECHLESS. Dunamis is even used across the New Testament 120 times! (Usually translated to "miracles," "works of power," "ability," or "strength!")

Here's what's going on in my head.

When we used to read this, we thought power; this strength, this ability, this supernaturalness of the Spirit to do things, so abstract yet sort of tangible. But really, it's "dunamis" or *dynamic*. Take the ideas that came to your head when I first asked what came to your mind and add the definitions that I've shown you. Now this is the power, the *dynamic* given to us, it is here! It should be overtaking all of who we are as children of God!

---

[9] Go back and read the definitions if you haven't already.

DYNAMIC: A CHRISTIAN FAITH

But how does this relate to God? I thought to myself that wherever something comes from, it must derive from something that is either that or more! This dunamis comes from the Holy Spirit, God's Spirit, God Himself. He is either *dynamic* or more! Whether you accept this or not, join me through the rest of my journey and thought processes before and after this discovery of whom I know God to be and hopefully you can get a glimpse of His beautiful *dynamic* within you!

CHAPTER 2:

THE MOVING SPIRIT OF GOD

DYNAMIC B.C. STORY

MORNING PRAYER

During my time at USC, I started to host a morning time of devotion and prayer every day at one of the chapels that we had. Every morning, at 8 am (now 9 am), I would invite people to join me in a time of devotion and solitude and then into a time of prayer together. At the beginning of the year, there was always a surplus of people due to the season of few responsibilities. One of the years, a now mentor of mine and Fuller Seminary student, Bekah Estrada came to join me in experiencing the space of the chapel.

I sat everyone who joined us down to talk about what we envisioned for what God had in store for us on campus that year. As we went around, I shared that I wanted to see more of the campus moving spiritually and in the surrounding community. Mind you, I had just gone through learning much about God's justice and reconciliatory work that we are all called to do through His love in us. Bekah shared that she wanted to see us just be anchored to our roots. The roots of our faith, to who God was. She had gone through a season of experiencing the beauty and wonders of God through a Catholic lens (not as a Catholic).

We started praying together and after Bekah finished praying about being anchored to our roots, and His word, I began to pray. As I was praying, I knew what Bekah was talking about and how it was something I knew God would desire of us, but I also knew that He would desire for us to be moving as well. To do justice, to love mercy, and to walk humbly with the Lord,[10] loving those around us by proclaiming good news, caring for the poor, freeing the oppressed, defending the cause and rights of the orphan and widow.[11] And so I prayed, asking God, how can it be possible that we are both moving and anchored? I thought of a ship being anchored and being able to move by possibly a long chain, but even then still bounded to the length of the chain.

So how is it possible? Praying, I continued my dialogue with God. Even when we're moving, it really is God's work within us that makes it possible. It is through His Spirit: Holy Spirit. Even without us, His Spirit can do the work that He wants to do. Then it was spoken, "God, let us be anchored to nothing else but your moving Spirit. Let us be anchored to the moving Spirit of God. In Jesus's name, Amen."

---

[10] Micah 8

[11] Isaiah 1:17, Psalm 82:3

2: THE MOVING SPIRIT OF GOD

WAIT WHAT? WHAT DOES THAT EVEN MEAN? I don't even know how that came to my mind, but I knew it was so full of the Spirit. My heart pounding, palms sweaty, mom's spaghetti. No. Really, what does that phrase mean? It sounded so profound and desirable to explore. Think about it with me.

ANCHORED TO THE MOVING SPIRIT OF GOD

First, is this even biblical? Good question. I looked around and did not find much other than some verses in Hebrews that used the word "anchor" metaphorically[12] to talk about the hope in the promises and unchanging character of God.

> "We have this as a sure and steadfast anchor of the soul, a hope that enters into the inner place behind the curtain, where Jesus has gone as a forerunner on our behalf, having become a high priest forever after the order of Melchizedek." (Hebrew 6:19 ESV)

This was only a single point in the Bible that would explicitly reference the idea of anchoring to God. Yet there are many other points in the Bible that while reading, you get the sense that He is inviting us to do similarly, to rest in Him,[13] or for Him to be our solid rock,[14] or to acknowledge and trust in Him.[15] We are constantly

---

[12] There are some verses in Acts that use anchor literally.

[13] Matthew 11:28-30

[14] Psalm 18:2

[15] Proverbs 3:5-6

DYNAMIC: A CHRISTIAN FAITH

shown that letting go of the control that we may have over any thing in our lives to Him would always result in the best for us.

When I began to meditate more on this phrase of "anchoring to His moving Spirit," I explored the idea that the only thing that we need to worry about is whether or not we're anchored, the rest of the work will be done with and through us. The weight and worry of the responsibility that comes with being a child of God should be nothing more than being solely focused on His Spirit given to you.

The picture I'm trying to paint here is that as we anchor to His moving Spirit, seek first His righteousness, His kingdom, and His heart; the rest that we need will be given to us.[16] Imagine what that looks like for you and Him. But again, what does that even mean?

Being anchored to something requires that we have first taken the step of faith and have begun to put all our focus on it. Focused enough that no matter where it flings us, we will never let go; whether it be down in the valleys or up on the peaks of our lives with our relinquish control over it. Almost like being on a rollercoaster.[17] An extreme one that needs one of those bars that comes over our head to hold us down to the seat in addition to the seat belt.

Are you ready to trust the Lord enough to let go of that control you have over something? To let go of your expectations

---

[16] Matthew 6:33

[17] Keyword, "Almost."

2: THE MOVING SPIRIT OF GOD

"ANCHORED" – TAYSHA KIM

of the outcomes or the experiences that you hope to have? Get on the ride. The ride of the life of the beloved. The ride that ends forever being anchored to the moving Spirit of God.

This is what I would call taking up the dynamic of the Holy Spirit. To allow Him to take over and take you freely through this life and all that you have been created for in the most creative and life-giving way.

ANCHORING

So what are these steps and ways of life that you are going to take? How do you anchor to the moving Spirit of God in every part of your life? Honestly, I'm still working on it myself and don't know all that it takes. What I do know are the first steps and the multiple processes that I have already done and tried.

1. *Identify Tendencies*
2. *Relinquish Expectations*
3. *Explore Disciplines*

1. *Identifying Tendencies*

Most of us don't notice, but we all have tendencies that are deeply rooted in our identity of the past. We need to be alert to identify them, especially ones that lead us away from the Spirit. Examples might include tendencies to worry, to withdraw, to over-share, to maintain distance, to risk, to avoid risk, to intellectualize, to sentimentalize, to stereotype, or to procrastinate.

2: THE MOVING SPIRIT OF GOD

For me, some of these tendencies might include trying to take control. Whether it be trying to get something that I want, or being a perfectionist to a fault, or trying to get everyone to do everything my way, or not letting down from an argument when I know of my "convictions", or even getting impatient when I'm the only one on time. Some of these could be reasoned as what you know as truths and essentials to life, but are really still forms of desires to control. Control can sometimes be helpful, but most of the time is a result of not trusting in God for whatever it is that we are facing.

When you get a chance, take some time to write out 3 tendencies that you have. It'll be good for you to be aware of them and in the future, to address when necessary.

2. Relinquishing Expectations

This one should be expected.[18] You need to begin to let go of the expectations that you have, especially the ones that are both unrealistic or not agreed upon by those involved. In our case, the majority of times, our expectations with God can be something we immaturely create without Him or is just an unrealistic or untrue expectation of who He is.

Common expectations that people hold with God that are untrue:

1.   *Nothing bad will happen to me if I am doing the work of God;*

---

[18] Get it? No? Ok.

DYNAMIC: A CHRISTIAN FAITH

2. *God will do what you want;*
3. *Only missionaries do missions;*
4. *God only uses Christians to do His work; and*
5. *God should speak to me in the way I want Him to.*

These tendencies or habits are not something that you can change in an instant. But for every instance that comes up when you have realized that you have set these expectations, take the time to wrestle against it. If you feel that you cannot do it alone (usually the case), invite others into the dialogue, especially God, about what you have been expecting and how it is both hurting others and a form of taking control; possibly not trusting in God.

3. Exploring Disciplines

Spiritual Disciplines have not only been the most common way to connect with God but also the most advocated within the Bible. I'm going to list a few of many spiritual disciplines that I have known of and used that you could remember for use in the future.

1. Sabbath – *Set apart a full day or 24-hour period to rest from what you have been doing the past 6 days. Use it to spend time with God.*

2. Morning Devotion & Prayer – *A dedicated amount of time in the morning intentionally spent in God's word and response to Him through prayer.*

3. Silence and Solitude – *Time set apart to intentionally be silent from your thoughts and surroundings, away from anyone and everyone.*

2: THE MOVING SPIRIT OF GOD

4. Brothers and Sisters in Christ – *Having a community of believers that are there whenever you need them and/or as you live life with them in faith.*

5. Musical Worship – *Listening or playing music with the intention of knowing and experiencing more of who God is through lyrics or music.*

6. Journaling – *Writing in a journal the thoughts that you have each day or the things you want to wrestle with. This is good for making your thoughts more concrete.*

7. Prayer Walk – *Walking around your neighborhood or the area and praying for it.*

8. Physical Discipline – *Your body is a temple of God! Taking care of it to keep it in its best condition through exercise and healthy diets.*

9. Meditation and Mindfulness – *Staying focused on being with God and others, by intentionally letting go of control in your mind to be more present or mindful of His Word.*

10. Recreational Activities – *Taking activities that have been life-giving or enjoyable to you and letting God reorient them towards Him. What that might look like. It may be different for each.*

11. Fasting – *Taking out a specific thing or activity out of your life, usually food, to be more focused and intentional with your relationship with God in humility.*

12. Rule of Life – *A contract that you place on yourself so that you may build habits into your daily life that would help order it to give out of a receiving posture from God. Inspired by Saint Benedict.*

DYNAMIC: A CHRISTIAN FAITH

In recent days, I've been using the discipline of memorizing God's word, through meditating on it day and night. It was nothing that I ever took as seriously as I am now. But in Psalms 1 it is mentioned that the one who delights in the law of the Lord, who meditates on it day and night is like a tree planted by streams of water. To me, it seems that this tree is one that is living its fullness with more than it can hope for. As I have begun my journey with a friend in memorizing the whole book of Psalms, I have never felt this feeling of being free and of peace. It's as if this type of meditation has made my spirit feel as if it were soaring, flying free through the life that I am living. But I have thought to myself, I have never really been one to stress or have much anxiety about anything in life. How is this any different than before? It's not like I've entered a higher dimension, it's just totally new and fuller. As I've struggled with trying to accurately describe this realization, nothing better has depicted this experience than the phrase of being anchored to the moving Holy Spirit of God.

Before, I walked freely without angst, fear, or stress. But now having anchored to the Holy Spirit, I am also focusing all of my mind and strength on being with Him through His word. As a result, I am not only experiencing freedom and peace, but also the wild adventure that the Holy Spirit is taking through my life and those around me. My hope, as my friend, Mike Parkyn[19] has reminded me, that it truly is the Holy Spirit, the moving one, that witnesses[20] through us.

---

[19] Same Mike from the first Chapter.

[20] John 15:26-27

CHAPTER 3:

PERFECT, NOT BALANCED

DYNAMIC B.C. STORY

I want to share this excerpt with you from one of my journal entries:

"The past few days have been enormous. Too much to comprehend, but I will still attempt to do so. Even though I planned my dates, I still haven't planned my days. I need to do work and I want to try my best. But I never know what's my best. Is it that I should allow for God's grace to overcome me? Or do I just not realize that security and keep going. God, please help me understand. It's so hard for me to stay balanced like the way you are. Though I don't think you're in balance. You're in perfection. It goes beyond a single state, into multiple states. Dynamic, not static. You move, that is one of your states. A moving one, that changes to your other states at the perfect time and for the perfect reason. Reveal more, O Lord."

DYNAMIC: A CHRISTIAN FAITH

I've thought about this for quite a while and have always focused on the part that I transitioned from God as one who was balanced to one who was perfect. But is there even a difference between perfection and balance? I believe so.

Using a two plate scale for example, balance is the steadiness of a position that, once found and held, all things involved can be held in equilibrium. Post-discovery of the equilibrium of a system, nothing needs to move, the most optimal position has been found. Perfection on the other hand can be a continuous action of switching from one side of a scale to the other creating a seemingly unmoving system yet with constant motion. Perfection includes continuous movement where balance does not.[21]

To take this further, balance is like lukewarm water, 50% cold and 50% hot all the time. Perfection is like water that is either 100% hot or 100% cold at the perfect time and for the perfect reason.

Even though I knew God was perfection my entire life, I am sure now that my perception of that perfection was really just an idea of balance. I thought that He was only this straight line that divided everything around into black and white. Something that He walked so tightly upon. It was either right or wrong. Holy or Sinful, Good or Evil, Big or Small, Love or Hate, God or Not, Truth or False.

---

[21] I include motion in perfection because it makes for a more dynamic definition and reality. But if you were to look into the existence of the reality of all objects, you will find that every solid object is really a bunch of very small particles moving at speeds that are not visible to the naked eye.

3: PERFECT, NOT BALANCED

"BALANCE VS. PERFECT" – MIKAYA KIM

DYNAMIC: A CHRISTIAN FAITH

"PERFECTLY TORN VEIL" – SAMUEL SUNITO

3: PERFECT, NOT BALANCED

Is He not those things? Is He not the one truth that is our solid rock? I believe He is, but what I've been conflicted about and hope to propose is that He is more than this dichotomy of black and white. He is this multi-faceted person who holds more than just a single personality unlike a one sided square, but rather on a different face for different reasons. At the very least He is three persons in one, unified. The Father, the Son, and the Holy Spirit.

PERFECT ACTION AT THE PERFECT TIME

To sum up what I'm sharing about here is that we see God always doing something different for different people, at different times, and for different situations. The same person going through the same situation twice at different times of their lifetime will be met with a different response from God. Two people going through the same situation at the same time will be met with a different action from God. I believe that God uniquely responds to each however He chooses. Whether it be through taking us through trials that are unbearable, or inviting us through seasons of blessings, or showing up in the smallest of ways, or through a miracle; He is still God despite how He might have done something outside of the character that we currently know Him to have.

God's unchanging character is full of different states. This even includes His emotions, allowing them to be felt and to be led by. What I mean is that sometimes He gets angry or wrathful, but He's not constantly in those states for we know He is also patient and merciful. This has led me to the different times in the Bible where God chose to do something different than what

He had intended or spoken to do as a result of one of His people requesting Him to do so. These include times like when God designed Adam and Eve for the Garden but then exiled them, was repentful or sorry for making humans,[22] asking Abraham to sacrifice his son,[23] destroying Sodom and Gomorrah,[24] telling Moses He will wipe all the Israelites except him,[25] destroying Nineveh,[26] on His way to heal Jairus' daughter,[27] turning water into wine,[28] or healing the servant of the centurion.[29] Not that He changed His will, but perhaps He changed His plan or had chosen to be interrupted or was responding to a changing person.

ILLUMINATING CONTRAST

A close friend of mine, Hannah Hiler,[30] shared this analogy with me as I was explaining this to her, making sense of a seemingly unchanging changing God.

> *"I think a color analogy would work well with this idea. Take the color orange. If you were to put it next to a cool, dark color like purple, the orange would feel and look brighter and warmer in contrast. But if you were to put that same orange next to a warm, lighter color like yellow,*

---

[22] Genesis 6:7

[23] Genesis 22:2

[24] Genesis 18:16-33

[25] Deuteronomy 9:13-14

[26] Jonah 3

[27] Luke 8:40-48

[28] John 2:1-11 Saying His time was not now, but still does it.

[29] Luke 7:1-10

[30] Another beloved sister in Christ that I met at USC who is very artistic.

3: PERFECT, NOT BALANCED

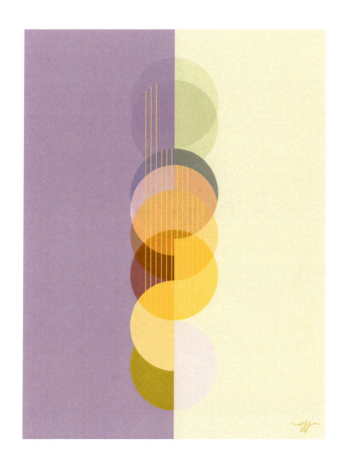

"STATICALLY DYNAMIC COLORS" - SHANNON JIANG

DYNAMIC: A CHRISTIAN FAITH

the orange would seem to lose its vibrancy. Although it is the same color, different aspects of that color come out in the different scenarios."

To put God through this perspective, He is like the color orange in this scenario, a constant color or person. Yet when in the presence of different colors or people, He looks different and is doing something different. His plan in those situations are different yet still align with His will and character of who He is. Maybe an interesting way to think about those situations in the Bible where God seems to have changed His mind, are really just the people changing in His presence. Their heart postures are changing and their faith increasing. As a result, God seems different yet He's only responding to this change by keeping His constant. An unchangeable changing being. Statically dynamic God. Perfect, not balanced. We're letting Him be yet understanding it will look different every time. The great I AM.

ILLUMINATING CONTEXT

One more example to drive home the idea of this perfection. What is being described above is similar to how most people read the Bible. When you read, you make sure that you take the CONTEXT into consideration. Without context, you can twist the Bible and its words to support you into doing anything! We've seen it happen before through the crusades, slavery, discrimination, oppression of the advocates, and much more. I'm sure this is something we have all learned while we have truly studied and meditated on the word of God. The context of the word we are reading is important, but so is the context in which we come to

— 30 —

3: PERFECT, NOT BALANCED

read it is as well. If we are to believe and communicate that God and His words are constantly not obsolete to the present, we need to understand that He is statically dynamic. The great I AM.

STATICALLY DYNAMIC

As people who desire God, seeking to be in continual relationship with Him, what does this understanding entail? Heart Posture. Increasing Humility, Creativity, and Change.

HUMILITY

This is very cliche but humility is the most necessary step for us to do anything good, really. We should always come with the mentality that we don't know everything and that we are not perfect, especially when coming before God. Even more so, the whole idea of God being dynamic is the understanding that we can't be too limiting of the ways that God interacts with others. If we are to do so, we are assuming that we have more power than God. I will reason that as co-heirs with Christ and of the dynamic of the Holy Spirit; with great power comes greater humility. Example, take time every morning to repent and to be more aware of the moments in which pride or ego arises. Address it. Constantly increase humility to be able to receive more of the fullness of His dynamic.

— 31 —

DYNAMIC: A CHRISTIAN FAITH

CREATIVITY

To begin a greater understanding of the perfect God, we
need to continually think out of the box. The box that we have
placed Him in, our logic, our minds, our theology. Though there
are certain core truths that we cannot contradict or veer off
from, we should still attempt to imagine the possibilities of
greater actions that come from letting different perspectives of
His character show. How, you ask? It could be moving to a distant
land away from relatives, or leading an oppressed people group
out of imprisonment, or taking out a goliath of an unethical
company, or calling out people who are hating and hurting others
under God's name, or allowing for the marginalized[31] to share
their story, or even writing into the future. People who I've seen
do such things include those of the prophets and forerunners of
our faith. Abraham, Moses, David, Isaiah, Daniel, Jesus,[32] John,
and the list goes on of whom have allowed creativity to stretch
their knowing and relationship with our Lord, God. They did and
allowed the unprecedented.

CHANGE

The way we live, the way we act, the way that we choose
to orient anything will ultimately affect our heart and mind.[33]
If we are to truly live out the truth that God is perfect, change

---

[31] This means that the majority was disregarding or mistreating a minority
group.

[32] Yes, I just called Jesus a forerunner of our faith in Himself.

[33] Mark 7:20-23

is necessary, for we will never perfectly know Him. To be more exact, change your heart posture. Find the real reason (pride, ego, selfishness, hate, anger, power, etc.) for why you're doing anything and ask God to reorder it for him. Without active changes in this, it could just be all thought and talk, not heart and walk. Creativity without active change is an illusion of pride within.

THE GREAT **I AM**

You might've noticed my reference to God as the great I AM. Moses asked Him,"Whom shall I say sent me when they ask?" God answers,"I AM who I AM."[34] I've always wondered what this could mean and I know some Christian theologians have done an excellent study of it. But I've always sat there thinking that God has named or described Himself so broadly. It was as if He tried to explain yet there was no other way but to use I AM. Similar to the word "good" when used to describe God. It's like when someone asks about how you and God are doing. So many things could have happened in the past month, week, or day. What more could you say other than He was and is "good?" Unless you're willing to talk for days. This attempt to describe Himself in the most concise and complete way was to say that He just Is. The present form of Himself. THAT CAN LITERALLY MEAN SO MANY THINGS! It's because He can choose to do anything yet He doesn't and if He were to describe it, it would have been so confusing. I'm here to formally propose the use of "dynamic" as near synonymous to "I AM who I AM." Taking the greek word, dunamis;

---

[34] Exodus 3:13-15

Dunamis = physical power, force, might, ability, efficacy, energy, meaning

He is physical power. He is force. He is might. He is ability. He is efficacy. He is energy. He is meaning. He is who He is. The Great I AM. Perfect, not Balanced.

CHAPTER 4:

FREEDOM IN STRUCTURE

DYNAMIC A.D. STORY

NOUN: DYNAMIC

The word "dynamic" was used in Acts 1:8 as a noun. "A force that stimulates change or progress within a system or process." The dynamic of the Holy Spirit to come upon us. This power of transformation, some of us would describe it as.

EXPERIENCING FAITH

Growing up in a predominantly Chinese and White Presbyterian church in the Los Angeles suburbs, for most of my life, the way that I saw faith and experienced it was so attached to my time spent there. I went to sunday schools right before our english service, went to the youth groups on Friday and hung out with friends in between or after. The way that I lived out my faith was only through the structures provided by the church that I attended. Every week was the same and everything I did was the same. Sometimes the content was different and the way it was delivered included a slight variation, but other than that, everything was the same. To me, nothing really differed from the people that went to church and the people that didn't. The city around our church was changing, the world around it was changing, but the church was not.

When I started at USC, I looked around all the different Christian fellowships. In the end I decided to stick with one. For the next few years I stayed involved with their ministry, taking part in their student leadership and endeavors to fulfill their mission of helping others on campus encounter Jesus and to love radically. Every week we had a large group where we would start with some ice breaker, then have worship, a speaker, and then close with response and worship and announcements. Every Sunday for the student leaders, we had meetings or workshops that we attended to learn more about living out our faith and leading Bible studies. Every year we grew, but every year we did similarly. The content was different and the way it was delivered sometimes included a variation, but other than that, every week was the same. To me, sometimes the way that some of the students lived that were in the fellowship compared to the students that were not did not differ much to me. The university was constantly changing and its students were adapting to the world that was spurring on ahead, but not the fellowship.

I'm not here to say that either was wrong or trying to paint them in an evil picture but what I do want to convey was that there was not much change amidst change around them.

TENSIONS

Over those years, I always felt tension with the way everything was done, from being in church to being in a fellowship and even hanging out with my friends in a Christian context. Sometimes there were events that were held out of the norm of what we did, those I desired. But the tension was that everything else felt boring, stagnant, lukewarm, or even dead. It felt as if we were doing everything out of tradition and had forgotten the reason why were doing any of these things, yet we were living it out in the context of faith. I don't know if this is something common around the country or world, I hope not, but I wonder, have you ever felt something like this? Some of us might call this complacency.

SHIFTING HISTORY

But was it just me desiring change? A desire for new things, a fresh breath of life and experiences to take hold of. When thinking about this, the history of Christian faith comes to my mind when I think about these tensions of desiring change in rigid environments or structures. In the context of the Bible, this faith in our God and the following of Jesus of a little over two thousand years ago, many changes and shifts have happened. From the beginning of time, to Moses, to the prophets, to Jesus, to the Roman Catholics, to the Reformation, to the Great Awakenings, to the Charismatics, and finally to the present, the faith of the millenials.

DYNAMIC: A CHRISTIAN FAITH

The theme I see across these times and events is the desire and power to change empowered by God. But every single time, the result was instead a desire to create a perfect structure that would be the most fruitful. As a result, they created rigid structures of fear. Fear of falling away from perfection. From Moses, a sacrificial structure of laws; from the prophets, the Pharisees and their oppressive Judaic structures; from Jesus, disciples that were hesitant to reach the Gentiles; from the Catholics, a need to pay for your sins; from the Reformation, communities of Protestant faith desiring only truth while forgetting love; the Great Revivals, structures to convert shallow faiths; and from the Charismatics, unhealthy desires of instant gratification of faith. **I'm not denouncing those events or people.** In fact, I am affirming God's work in every one of them. God leading the Israelites out of slavery, prophets speaking God's heart of justice, Jesus living out God's radical love, Roman Catholics bringing the beauty of Our Savior, the Reformed desiring the roots of faith, the Great Awakenings realizing the urgency of the Great Commission, and the Charismatics living out of the Holy Spirit. But now, I believe that we are back to idolizing these structures or strategies in which we use to seek, follow, and love Jesus.

Arguably, structures are great! They provide for the stability of efficiency, effectiveness, and growth. It's irresistible! Especially if you have a structure already in place, it's not like you can liquify it and create a new one! I remember exploring the idea of just demolishing all the structures that exist and wondering if that would be much better than having such rigid and repressive environments for people to reside in. I concluded with the fact that chaos would only ensue.

— 38 —

4: FREEDOM IN STRUCTURE

So what am I alluding to? Is there a solution? Is there something that we can do? I believe there is a way that we can utilize structure yet not let our idolization of it prevent us from fully living out this change that Jesus has intended for us since the beginning. Just like the title of this chapter, a freedom in structure.

What does this mean you may ask? I'm talking about creating a structure that changes within itself rather than just the content where the way that anything is done is according to the season or environment that one is in, a dynamic structure. But how do you create something like that? Excellent question! I'm glad you asked! Asking is already more than half the battle! Maybe I'll just stop here and let you and your community figure that out on your own. It's not like I know all the answers.[35]

ESSENTIALS VS. NON-ESSENTIALS

But first you might ask, isn't this risky for those whom we are trying to lead with these structures? If something is too volatile, we might easily create structures of evil, falsehood, and unproductiveness! You are correct in implying so!

It is important for the structure to be created within a common faith or set of beliefs! Ones that hold the foundation of which to build upon. That is why I believe that these structures of freedom must be created within the context of our Christian

---

[35] No, like seriously, I don't! Haha!

— 39 —

DYNAMIC: A CHRISTIAN FAITH

faith. Even those that were being sent to call out the falsehood of a structure or to bring about change, always came from a desire of bringing them back to the fulfillment of their roots. I'm referring to the history of Christian catalysts of God I mentioned earlier.

The funny thing is, in our faith, there are countless things that people divide themselves over. Most of them are commonly thought of as controversial topics. So amongst all these differing beliefs, how can you continue?

I believe the only way you can get through this is to begin, if you haven't yet, to think about the core truths that make up our faith, the essentials. Explore them and set those apart from every other part of the belief, just like how Paul decided he would go to the Gentiles and Peter to the Jews and that circumcision wasn't essential to faith.[36] Let these truths be the guide in which you create your structure.

CONTINUOUS CHANGE, ACTIVITY OR PROGRESS

Once you're finished, always ask yourself these questions to help assess whether or not your structure allows for freedom.

1. If you already have an existing structure, does your structure change from time to time or has it been the same since its conception? Not that this is bad, but could make for a good indicator of need of movement as a group.

---

[36] Galatians 2

4: FREEDOM IN STRUCTURE

"FREEDOM IN STRUCTURE" - THERESA LI

DYNAMIC: A CHRISTIAN FAITH

2. What is the purpose of your structure? If it is for a general belief, then create new structures within this one that have more specific purposes to the season, activity, or area of growth. (Ex. "Our purpose is to love Jesus." Let this be an outer structure, and create a new one that's more specific. "As a church we will serve a specific people group as we grow together.")

3. Is there a process that encourages change in your structure or creation of ones within? Be assured to have this, because without it, you will find change extremely difficult to bring.

4. When people voice genuine concern against your structure, do you consider or brush them off? Pride is the #1 enemy to God, because it is what creates stubbornness to His change and movement within and around.

But maybe you believe you already have the foundations of faith, then what I'm challenging you to see is not that your foundation is flawed but that the structure in which you implement it is too shallow. It seems that the majority sees and lives in a 2D fashion. The boundaries and foundations have been set, but what is missing is the actual building or vessel that would give its height and depth to increase the glory of their faith. Perspective, experience, character, discipline, emotional maturity, love, etc.; any number of these could be missing.

I'll close with an image of a flexible-like container with some water enclosed within. Creating a structure of freedom requires that we only need to create a big and flexible enough container so that the contents within can move and become freely, from

— 42 —

4: FREEDOM IN STRUCTURE

water to gas, to ice or more, especially in this image. Freedom in structure. If your structure is too rigid, like a glass square, it would be difficult for your contents to become free, to come alive. The water would have a difficult time expanding, the gas too compact to move around, and the water limited a square shape.

Use that creativity of yours that God has given you and try a different and new thing with the same faith, the same purpose, and the same dynamic!

CHAPTER 5:

DYNAMIC SPIRITUAL DISCIPLINES

DYNAMIC A.D. STORY

DEAR, MAYBE SPIRITUALLY STAGNANT

Spiritual Disciplines are well known ways of practicing one's faith in the Christian life: from Bible reading, to praying, to fasting, to worship. There are many more well known disciplines, but I am not here to delve into them, especially where other communicators of faith do better. Instead, I invite you to think about the implications of the word dynamic in our spiritual lives through our disciplines. I believe this requires that we start with understanding ourselves more as creation.

DYNAMIC: A CHRISTIAN FAITH

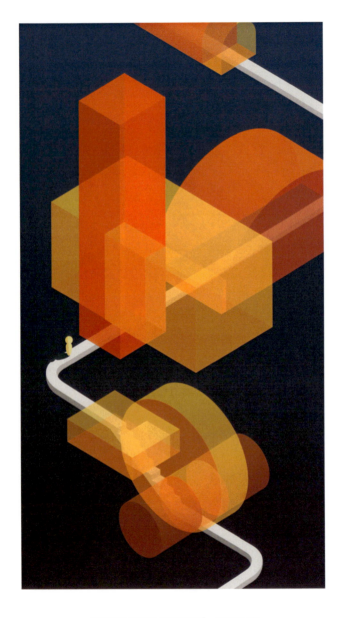

"IN THE MIDST OF IT ALL" – EMILY LU

5: DYNAMIC SPIRITUAL DISCIPLINES

SEASONS

As humans, made to exist in a world that has changing seasons, we are subjected to seasons.[37] By seasons, I mean periods of time where a certain aspect of your life has become a focus. Whether it be a feeling, a specific event, a challenge, or even a person that affects who you are for that period of time, lasting from a few days to a few months or a few years. Think about it, what is the focus of your current season today?

You might be in a season of learning patience. A season of mourning. A slow season in your career. A season of moving churches. A season of joy. A season of settling in as a family with a newborn. A flourishing season with God. Possibly all of those seasons together. So what season are you really in? Confusing right? What I'm trying to point out is that there could possibly be layers of seasons. Ones that pertain to different parts of who you are and your life. These can include your character, feelings, career, relationships, and spirituality,[38] each with their own rhythms. This can vary in amounts of seasons (ex. four or five season), length of periods (ex. three or four months), and intensity.

So what does this have to do with spiritual disciplines or our desire to seek God? As a farmer if your land was in the season of harvest, your discipline would be to reap. If it were in the season of sowing, your discipline would be to sow seeds. If it were in the season of sabbath, your discipline would be to rest and worship.

---

[37] Ecclesiastes 3 & Psalms 1

[38] Possibly more, but who am I to know them all.

DYNAMIC: A CHRISTIAN FAITH

Your seasons determine which disciplines you should exercise. You wouldn't reap during a time of sowing would you? The field would be empty! You wouldn't sow during a time of harvest, would you? There would be no space! Again, your seasons determine which disciplines you should exercise. Consistency is good and anchoring for hard seasons, but during different seasons you could easily become complacent and possibly a "righteous" person, not desiring change.

"Don't you think that we should always read the Bible and Pray though, Enoch? What do you mean, that we should do differently? The word of God is truth, how can you depart from such things?" That's true! What I'm proposing is not the idea of departing from these core disciplines but to reorient the ways that you use and do them in your different seasons. In some seasons, you could focus on reading the word; in others, meditate or memorize, or share it even! There are so many other ways to utilize these core tools of faith! Be creative about using them in the different seasons of any area of life.

What seasons are you in right now? Are your disciplines appropriate for the seasons you're in? Do your prayers reflect the season you're in, is it too risky for any other prayer?

IDENTIFYING SEASONS

It is important that you are able to identify what season you're in, especially when you're in a season of dryness. To be able to recognize that you're in that season will help you discern

— 48 —

5: DYNAMIC SPIRITUAL DISCIPLINES

"LAYERED SEASONS" – BREANNA DE VERA

how you should respond and worship. To know what season you're in will help combat the disappointment and discouragement that you might set yourself up with by thinking you're in an entirely different season. But how do you identify what season you're in? Just like the way you identify the seasons of the calendar, so can you in your life! Sometimes, it may seem obvious like the fact that you are moving to another place, or starting a new job or shift. But others are not, like what part of your character is God pruning right now, or how should you be growing in and through your marriage or friendships? I'll share with you some of my experiences and how I have navigated through identifying seasons. So far, I have used three identifiers:

1. Big Events
2. Small Things
3. Bodily Responses

1. Big Events

These should be simple to find. They're so big that when they come, you are stopped dead in your tracks. This could be a death of a loved one, a loss of employment, or a mid-life crisis. But they can also be good things as well! Examples like, getting married, having a newborn, or getting a promotion or a raise even. All can be helpful in identifying what season you're in. Acknowledging that it happened can help you realize that you're at least entering into a different season than what you have been in before.

Recently, I started an internship that required working 8 hours a day. Before, my disciplines would include an hour of

5: DYNAMIC SPIRITUAL DISCIPLINES

quiet time in the morning and a 5 minute read of a psalm at night. Now, because of my time commitment and need to allot time to commute to work, I read a psalm three times a day with a few minutes to reflect and pray as well. My sabbaths used to include spending time with people because I lacked previously, but now because of work, sabbaths are a dedication to silence and solitude. This new season of work was an indicator that I needed to change my disciplines.

Another personal example was during the time that I had first started driving. Because of my car I was getting everywhere quickly. I wanted to be on time and I wanted to beat traffic. As a result, I would drive recklessly especially when in a rush. One of the times I was driving in a rush to run some errands, I got in a car crash. I attempted to make a close turn but failed. Immediately I knew that I had been impatient and that it was time for me to learn more about patience especially with God. I know it looks like I made too quick of a judgement but that was not the only reason why.

2. The Small Things

At church a week before, the sermon was about patience and so was the Bible study that I was attending at a separate ministry. I noticed that patience was a topic of multiple conversations between my friends and I. The Christian radio I was listening to had themes of patience. I was frustrated with the people around me who couldn't get to places on time or even respond. I was sitting in rush hour angry. My heart was just impatient. I was impatient. All these things could have gone over my head had I

DYNAMIC: A CHRISTIAN FAITH

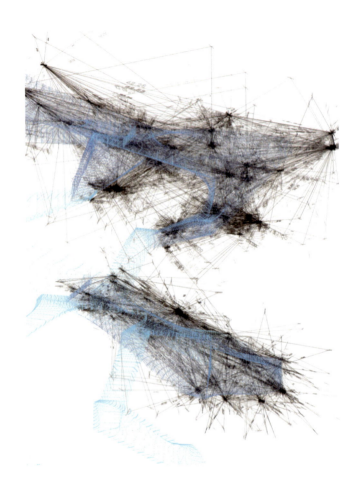

"CLOUDGRAFT" – JASPER LEONG

5: DYNAMIC SPIRITUAL DISCIPLINES

"CLOUDGRAFT" – JASPER LEONG

DYNAMIC: A CHRISTIAN FAITH

not taken those moments to sit and reflect on what was going
on. For me, I journaled these thoughts. The day of my car crash,
I took time to look back at my journal and found my reflections. I
definitely was in a season of learning patience.

3. Bodily Responses

Have you heard of the caution, "Be careful of what you pray
for?" For me, this always pertained to prayers like "God, would
you make me more patient?" or "Humble me, God." Most of the
time, you know that when you pray this you're about to make
your life a mess. God loves to answer these prayers and I believe
that when you pray these types of prayers, you'll definitely enter
into a season of that area.

In the past month, I was finishing the season of self-control.
From it, I learned the limitlessness of placing healthy limits or
boundaries on your life and that self-control was not moderation.
I then voiced to God in prayer and journal entry that I desired to
let go more of my control of my life. I wanted His Holy Spirit to
truly guide my life and that I wanted no control over it. As you
might be thinking, I then began to enter into a season of losing
control.[39] That week, I started losing control over everything.
From my job, to my passions, my sins, my character, my friendships, everything. My stomach was uneasy. My heart was beating
too quickly. My nervous system failed to provide me stability and I
began to lose feeling in my fingers and legs. For a few days it was
almost paralyzing. I felt so much anxiety when usually amongst

---

[39] Fun, right?

— 54 —

these occurrences in any other circumstance I would have been very carefree and relaxed about. This was not the first time, nor will it be my last. I have felt this emotion for what seemed as almost no reason many times, but as I reflect on them now, were only cases of transitioning or entering into new seasons.

Just like the events that precede the seasons of this world, where animals begin to migrate, the flowers begin to bloom, and the leaves begin to fall, we can reflect on them to realize the season that is to come. What about you? What are some unusual bodily responses that come about during times of difficult transition or change?

P.S.

How does this relate to dynamic? Having a more dynamic faith to live with a dynamic God requires that we understand that we are context and time constrained beings. Due to the fact that we are bound to both time and situation, we must allow the transformation of the way we live out faith within those bounds; different each time.

The way that we must live out these spiritual disciplines, must we also live out the purpose of our lives. I believe that with each season there comes a different purpose for our life. This might sound ridiculous but our purposes for each season are just the dynamic applications of the overarching mission of our lives. For me, it is to love God and to love those around me as I myself am. But more specific, my purpose now is to write this book, to go to work, and to finish school.

CHAPTER 6:

GOD'S PLAN

DYNAMIC A.D. STORY

CHAPTER OUTLINE

Remember, this is an invitation to explore, to challenge and stretch what you know. There are three things I want to explore in this chapter and I will let you know now because it's a little thicker by content than most chapters because they pertain to freewill and predestination.

1. *Faith vs. Grace*
2. *Forthtelling vs. Foretelling*
3. *God's Will vs God's Plan*

FAITH SANDWICHED BY GRACE

"For by grace you have been saved through faith. And this is not your own doing; it is the gift of God, not a result of works, so that no one may boast." (Ephesians 2:8-9 ESV)

DYNAMIC: A CHRISTIAN FAITH

For me, this verse was taught to me in a very clouded way. The grace part and the faith part of this process were taught as inseparable. If you were to ever talk about being saved, it was assumed that you had made a decision of faith. But. By grace? I was still confused. So by grace you were given faith to be saved? The order in which grace and faith happened was confusing for me. On one hand, you being saved had nothing to do with your choice because faith was given to you by grace from God. So, me being saved has nothing to do with my choice in following Jesus? On the other, I read that Jesus always spoke of the idea that we had to make the choice of faith ourselves.[40] But which is it? That we have a choice? Or that we don't have a choice, but it is through faith? Looking back, what Paul shares here in these few verses is that once there is faith, by grace you are saved. Meaning if you don't have faith, then there is no grace to be saved by. But still, I am sure there is grace even outside of faith. How does God's grace apply outside of faith? After thinking about this more, I concluded. I believe that there is grace that has been given to us and that it is the opportunity to choose into faith, to then be predestined to be saved by grace.

Grace of Choice >> Faith >> Grace of Salvation

What I'm trying to point out is that predestination happens within faith and His pursuit of grace for us. It is to be predestined with God in eternity. Outside of this faith, there is no predestination. I say there is just chaos outside of faith because there is no plan for those who have chosen to follow their own. But in the

---

[40] Matthew 7:13-29

context of our faith, everyone is imperfect and the only other way to have a chance of salvation is to be perfect. Thus, you can say there is predestination out of faith, and that is the eternity apart from the presence of God, Hell. Paul writes that we, referring to those in faith, have been chosen in Him.

> "*Blessed be the God and Father of our Lord Jesus Christ, who has blessed us in Christ with every spiritual blessing in the heavenly places, even as* **he chose us in him** *before the foundation of the world, that we should be holy and blameless before him. In love he predestined us for adoption* **to himself as sons through Jesus Christ**, *according to the purpose of his will, to the praise of his glorious grace, with which he has blessed us in the Beloved." (Ephesians 5:3-6)*

To those that have chosen to be in Him have then been called to be holy and blameless. This was decided before the foundation of the world. How does this all relate to the dynamic of God? I'll talk about it in a bit.

SPEAKING WITH AUTHORITY, FORTHTELLING

After integrating more of dynamic into my definition of faith, one of the topics that popped up in my reading and conversations was through this verse:

> "*And God said, 'Let there be light,' and there was light."*
> *(Genesis 1:3 ESV)*

DYNAMIC: A CHRISTIAN FAITH

The question that I asked myself was, "Did God know there was going to be light before He said 'Let there be light?' Or 'Because of God's power through His words light came to be?'" I thought about it for a little while and I reasoned that the ability to foreknow what was to come, was one that was less powerful than being able to cause, create, and change with mere words and thought. To me, it is more dynamic that He is able to create versus just to know. I know you have a lot of questions and criticisms about how I ironically asked a static question. Finish this chapter as a whole!

Words of Eternity

The thing is, we know that God is all-knowing and all-powerful. Despite the fact that His words bring forth the existence of its purpose, He also knew that they would come. But I reason that because of His power and authority, He knows whatever He desires will always come into fruition. As the perfect being that He is, His words hold perfect authority. His ability to forthtell, to speak things into existence, makes Him seem like He is foretelling when really it's both. Especially with the instance of the resurrection of Jesus after His death on the cross. This was spoken of starting in Genesis 3 through all of the Old Testament and from Jesus Himself. But the power of God's words were not just of the power to raise the dead or to pay for all sins, but I suggest, **to change eternity**. Right before the moment of Jesus' death, eternity existed with us not being able to dwell with God. There was no other way, but once He died and was resurrected, eternity was changed. Now, out of His power and grace, we now can have the opportunity to dwell with Him for eternity.

— 60 —

6: GOD'S PLAN

His words hold this power, ***the power to change eternity***. When answering the Sadducees' question, Jesus alluded to this power.

> "But Jesus answered them, **'You are wrong, because you know neither the Scriptures nor the power of God. For in the resurrection they neither marry nor are given in marriage, but are like angels in heaven. And as for the resurrection of the dead, have you not read what was said to you by God: "I am the God of Abraham, and the God of Isaac, and the God of Jacob"? He is not God of the dead, but of the living.'"** (Matthew 22:29-32)

The Sadducees were mistaken about the resurrection. The focus is not about the resurrection itself, but of the being and power behind it. The greek word used here, translated to power, is the word dunamis. God is the God of the living, of the dynamic. They did not understand God's dynamic. If anything, you can look at it as the power of resurrection as the bringing up of those who were alive. Those who lived with and within the dynamic of God. A stretch of this could be the two people in the Bible who never had to experience death, Enoch and Elijah. Their ascendence could be a foreshadow for those who walked with God. God did not raise them from the dead but rather took them in as they lived in faith. In His dynamic. In His power. In His love. With all of this as my conclusion, this changes the way that we should think about every other time we see God speaking, especially through His leaders and prophets of the faith.

DYNAMIC: A CHRISTIAN FAITH

Power vs. Authority

When we look at the times God spoke to His leaders in the Old Testament, from Adam and Eve,[41] Noah,[42] Abraham and Sarah,[43] Isaac and Rebekah,[44] Jacob,[45] Moses,[46] to David,[47] and others, everything said to them always happened and were true. Even when we look to Psalms, Isaiah, Zechariah, and other prophets, where it is the prophets speaking on behalf of God, many of their words have now been fulfilled, but not all of it. It seems as if His people, the prophets of God, were given the power to forthtell, **to change eternity**. In the end, these conversations of changing eternity lead to the Garden of Eden, where God gave Adam and Eve free will. Out of that, they changed eternity and were exiled from the Garden. That is where it all began. The eternity of humanity changed, by the hands of His people.[48] They changed their own eternities. The same for us, we have our own eternity in our hands. We can either choose into or out of faith, but as a result could influence the eternity of those that surround us as well.

I then raised some questions, "What then differentiates His people from Him? What makes God, God? And us His people, His creation?" At the very least, as creations made in His image, we

---

[41] Genesis 3:15-20

[42] Genesis 6:9

[43] Genesis 15:4

[44] Genesis 25:23

[45] Genesis 28:10

[46] Exodus 3: 21-23

[47] 2 Samuel 7:12-16

[48] Genesis 3

have this power, but God Himself holds all authority and power, perfect sovereignty.[49] Perfect in His Will, all of His desires are true and come about through His authority. If He wants something done, it will happen. But us in our imperfection outside of His Will, would not have all our desires fulfilled. We don't have the same authority, but we have the same power. The reason being is that we only have authority in and through the life of Jesus and His lordship over our lives. The times and areas where we do not decide to surrender to Him, we do not sit in His authority.

But why would God give us this power? We might never know, but I'd like to think that He'd prefer people who would make genuine choices to be in relationship with Him than to be manipulated to. Relationships are two way, if we want to communicate that this faith is a relationship more than it is a man-made religion, then we're going to need to believe it holistically. Hopefully, this would also change the way we see relationships here on earth, both how we treat and how we build one another up.

THE EXECUTION OF HIS WILL

The most common way that I have seen people describe God statically is through the notion of God's plan. That everything is planned out for you or that every single move you make is calculated and foreseen by God. I'm not saying that it's not Biblical and true, but what is for sure is that it is a very static

---

[49] Matthew 28:18-20 - Yes there's a difference. The word authority is a different greek word than power.

DYNAMIC: A CHRISTIAN FAITH

description and view of God's power. These ideas usually play out in forms like this:

1. *God has a plan and a purpose for you.*
2. *He has predestined who goes to Heaven and who goes to Hell out of grace.*
3. *He is all-knowing and all-loving and because He wants the best for us, He has already influenced your life in such a way that everything you do is really not your choice.*
4. *Don't worry, everything has been worked out for your own good. Where you are now is where you are supposed to be.*
5. *It is out of grace that you have been given faith to be saved.*
6. *He knows all that is going to happen so it means He must have a plan.*

How is this a static view of God's plan and possibly His power? The statement I especially want to challenge is that "He knows all that is going to happen so it means He must have everything planned out." When you think of something that is planned out, it means that it won't change. Especially in the case of God who is all-powerful, it must mean that it will all go according to plan, to what has been decided. It doesn't move and has no room for it to be different, to be alive. But the problem that I have with this is the assumption that an all-powerful and all-knowing God must have a plan for everything to go the way that He desires.

But what does God desire? Does what He desire require that everything goes according to a single plan? When we begin asking the question of what does God desire, it shifts our questions

— 64 —

6: GOD'S PLAN

away from "what is God's plan" to "what is God's will?" There is a difference between a plan and a will. A plan is where everything is managed at the micro level. Everything is set to happen a specific way and there is no deviation. A will is instead on the macro level where it is the ideas and deepest yearnings of the heart and mind. God's Will = God's Heart. But God does have a plan, right? I mean there's all these verses that allude to the fact that He has a plan!

"For I know the plans I have for you, declares the Lord, plans for welfare and not for evil, to give you a future and a hope." (Jeremiah 29:11)

"This Jesus, delivered up according to the definite plan and foreknowledge of God, you crucified and killed by the hands of lawless men." (Acts 2:23)

"And we know that for those who love God all things work together for good, for those who are called according to his purpose. For those whom he foreknew he also predestined to be conformed to the image of his Son, in order that he might be the firstborn among many brothers." (Romans 8:28-29)

Its partially true. For me to read these in the context of where they came from, I believe that these are for those that have chosen in Him. For Jeremiah, God was speaking to Israel, the people whom He chose but also chose Him as well. Luke, writing in Acts above, talks about the instances that God has chosen to plan something. It was a definite plan that existed for the sake of a purpose. The word definite here means that there are boundaries of this plan. What I mean is that this plan could have been executed in any other time period but it was instead chosen here. For Paul, I ask the question, "Who does God not foreknow? Is He incapable of

DYNAMIC: A CHRISTIAN FAITH

foreknowing everyone?" I believe that Paul writing this in Romans was in the context for those who have chosen to love God.

So what does this really mean for us? From this, I am not trying to say there is something monumental that must change, rather I hope that this mindset and understanding would change the way that we respond to those that feel that everything is against them, even God. In the end, there is a grace of choice. This grace given to us to have the freedom of choosing into God. Once we choose, there is the grace of salvation that inevitable takes us to eternity with God. But included in this choice, you are also choosing into the plan that God has predestined for you. You are accepting and desiring His complete lordship by total surrender to His Will and purpose for you. His perfect and good purpose for you. But outside of this choice, the choice away from Him, you will find yourself in your own imperfect plan. One that will only but lead to your own demise in eternal separation from Him.

PRAYER

So how do all these topics work together? Within this entire conversation, the one thing that we have been missing is the importance of prayer. One of the most crucial and dynamic parts of our faith is prayer, the medium that God invites us into with Him. Many times when we talk about these topics, we forget about the fact that God invites His people to talk with Him, to commune with Him. He desires that we be honest with Him amidst our struggles, confusion, and inability to know and control all things.[50]

---

[50] The Book of Job

6: GOD'S PLAN

He invites us to ask as His children, depicting Himself as the loving Father that would open, provide, reveal, and rejoice.[51]

Prayer and Faith vs. Grace

The combination of God's grace, God's pursuit, and our faith paints the picture of a complete relationship of love. It is only but a small glimpse into the commune of the Father, the Son, and the Holy Spirit. God desires for us to experience the fullness that He has in Himself with His community. He provides prayer as the gateway to experience this overwhelming perfect love. Through prayer, we can make the choice of faith within His grace, grace of choice and grace of salvation.

Prayer and Forthtelling vs. Foretelling

Through prayer, we are given this access to power and authority through the Holy Spirit to change eternity with Him. We get to work with Him in completing His wonderful work of loving His people and intervening in His creation towards shalom. We can use prayer to build and encourage one another in faith, forth telling the hope of their future, healing their hurts of the past, and their present and eternal life with God. Through prayer, we can help others receive the dynamic that was behind the resurrection of Jesus to walk in a constantly transforming life of love and grace.

---

[51] Luke 11:9-13

Prayer and God's Will vs. God's Plan

The dynamic of God's plan includes the juxtaposition of His Will, His Grace, and His Love. They all work together in giving us this image of God who is alive. Who is constantly working. Who is constantly watching and waiting for us to respond to His work in and around us. He is waiting for you to step into this dynamic relationship with Him. Prayer is the most important way we can respond to the invitation and power of His Word. Prayer is the way we can constantly work towards surrendering all parts of our plan to His Will so that He can make us a fuller image of Himself, of His Son Jesus as part of His body. This relationship with Him through prayer and life is what gives us a more dynamic view of God's plan.

CHAPTER 7:

COMPLETE IMAGES OF GOD

DYNAMIC A.D. STORY

WARNING – *this is going to be an intense chapter*

QUICK OUTLINE

Applying the implications of dynamic faith to our views of God and of people while seeking understanding of how to respond to those implications.

I. Our Image of God
II. Our Image of Ourselves - as People (His Creation)

I. OUR IMAGE OF GOD

We're imperfect people. The fact that we can make mistakes is evident of our shortcomings. But the Bible even talks about the ways that we fall short of everything that God desires of us.[52] One of these ways I want to delve into is the way that we view Him. I want to bring up an idea to challenge the way that we currently see Him and while hopefully being short and to the point.

God of Limits

I've never been taught this so bear with me as I try to explore this part of who God is. I don't know if you've ever thought of this, but I've always found it intriguing to see God limit Himself in the Bible. At least, that's the way that I have seen it. I'll share with you three ways that I've seen God do this in the Bible and why I perceive it like that.

God's Character and Covenants

I guess you can say that this could be a very self-evident fact of who God is. God does not lie. If anything, He is truth itself. It's almost as if He cannot be anything else. This is something that is innately part of who He is, so some would argue that it's not a form of limiting Himself. Though I would try to argue that God chooses to be Truth rather than just allowing the fact that He is.

The following passage that I'm going to share with you is of a psalm about the relationship between God and David. God speaking,

> "I will not violate my covenant or alter the word that
> went forth from my lips. Once for all I have sworn by my

---

[52] Romans 3:23

7: COMPLETE IMAGES OF GOD

holiness; I will not lie to David. His offspring shall endure forever, his throne as long as the sun before me. Like the moon it shall be established forever, a faithful witness in the skies."
(Psalm 89:34-37 ESV)

We see that God limits Himself when He establishes a covenant with those whom He loves. In this case, God made a covenant with David to never alter His words and neither to lie. But this is not the first time we've seen God make promises. At the very beginning, God does similarly when He restarts His creation with Noah.

"I establish my covenant with you, that never again shall all flesh be cut off by the waters of the flood, and never again shall there be a flood to destroy the earth." And God said, "This is the sign of the covenant that I make between me and you and every living creature that is with you, for all future generations: I have set my bow in the cloud, and it shall be a sign of the covenant between me and the earth."
(Genesis 9:11-13 ESV)

Again, God makes a covenant with Noah and with all of His creation that He would never flood the earth by water to destroy it. God is vowing that water would never be the end of all His creation. I find this to be an incredible statement from God. If He were ever to destroy the earth again, He will have to use some other method. He's almost forcing Himself to be creative by limiting the ways that He would have to use if it were necessary.

— 71 —

DYNAMIC: A CHRISTIAN FAITH

The Execution of the Salvation Plan

A more explicit version of how God chooses to limit Himself can be seen through the way that He executes His salvation plan post "The Fall" in Genesis. Jesus, His son, descends onto the earth from His Heavenly realm. Now obliged to live in a human form until the day of salvation and His death. Paul extrapolates,

> "Have this mind among yourselves, which is yours in Christ Jesus, who, though he was in the form of God, did not count equality with God a thing to be grasped, but **emptied himself**, by taking the form of a servant, being born in the likeness of men. And being found in human form, he humbled himself by becoming obedient to the point of death, even death on a cross."
> (Philippians 2:5-8 ESV)

Jesus, who is God, relinquished that form and instead chose to be human. He took this opportunity to become what was needed in order to fulfill the plan of salvation. It took limiting Himself into human form and taking up the limitations that people experience when apart from the presence of God. Some might argue that this is something that is impossible for God to do, but we see that Jesus had to fulfill this plan in this way, even when it wasn't part of His will.[53] Yet the existence of this plan in which there was no other way, in of itself was a form of limiting Himself. God can save everyone in an instant, providing salvation any other way, yet He chose this one.

---

[53] Matthew 26:39, Mark 14:26, Luke 22:42, John 12:27

7: COMPLETE IMAGES OF GOD

His Mercy

But the most interesting way that I've seen God limit Himself is through His blotting of people, events, or things from His memory. Isaiah, the prophet, brings forth the word of God,

> "I, I am he who blots out your transgressions for my own sake, and I will not remember your sins." (Isaiah 43:25 ESV)

God is speaking of the wretchedness of His people, Israel, and how they do not even desire of Him. Yet His mercy is here and His intolerance for sin is apparent. He is more than willing to blot out, to completely abolish, from His memory all the evil and spite of Israel against Him. His anger boils against their hard hearts and stiff-neck minds.[54] Similarly, it has bled out before Moses at the peak of their foolishness in the form of even blotting them out of the Book of Life.

> "The next day Moses said to the people, 'You have sinned a great sin. And now I will go up to the LORD; perhaps I can make atonement for your sin.' So Moses returned to the LORD and said, 'Alas, this people has sinned a great sin. They have made for themselves gods of gold. But now, if you will forgive their sin—but if not, please blot me out of your book that you have written.' But the LORD said to Moses, 'Whoever has sinned against me, I will blot out of my book.'" (Exodus 32:30-33 ESV)

This eternal book, presumably the Book of Life, is seen with the possibility of being edited by the Lord. God desires and is able to blot out those who are against Him, those in sin. This extreme

---

[54] Exodus 33:5

— 73 —

form of forgetting and abolishing sin from His presence is part of who God is. He has chosen that this is how He responds but more so, this is how He has placed limits upon Himself for His own sake[55] and of those whom He loves.

Entailment of God Who Limits

Why at all is this important to think about? The reason I bring this up is because of what this might entail for our faith. If God is one who is constantly interacting with His creation in this way as a result of limiting Himself, then we might need to begin challenging the way that we see Him in every other way. Not to say that we are false in the way that we see Him, but that it is possible that we might have an incomplete image of who He is due to our complacency or misconception of Him now.[56] The reality of this is that there is a continual realization that we must have, that we have incomplete images of who God is. Without this, we will always find ourselves amongst a faith that is attempting the idolization of an image that we have built, a simple golden calf religion. Without this, we will always be met with people who will take our incomplete images and attempt to bring in false parts of who God is, making it possible for either parties to lead astray others of the faith and of the lost. Having a dynamic, continually changing and progressing, image of who God is will leave no room for the misleading ideas of this world but will instead, bring ever-increasing glory, glory to God. A dynamic knowing of God for a dynamic relationship.

---

[55] This refers to God not tolerating any sin in His presence.

[56] Though some might argue that this also means false.

7: COMPLETE IMAGES OF GOD

I. OUR IMAGE OF OURSELVES

Before I continue the rest of this chapter, I want to remind you that what I write is not law. It does not assume power over anything or anyone. I'm merely speculating the possibilities of what faith might begin to look like if it were to consider dynamic as part of its fullest meaning.

Placing Star People in Square Boxes

A common theme that has arisen in some societies of this world include this realization that people, especially children, should not be judged by what we deem natural or given. You will always find a fish failing if you judge it by how high it can climb a tree. Not everyone is good at math, or science, yet a majority of this world assumes this position when educating the masses. As a result, victims of this mentality have been labeled incompetent or unworthy, making it near impossible for them to thrive in the environment that they reside in. But I'm sure that this theme did not come out of nowhere. Deep within the hearts of people lives this discomfort of the constructs of societies and systems, how they are not the way that they should be.

If you looked at the beginning, people were made to exist in a world that flowed and interacted perfectly.[57] People were made in the image of God, in likeness of Him.[58] But now we live in a

---

[57] Genesis 1:31

[58] Genesis 1:27

DYNAMIC: A CHRISTIAN FAITH

world of tainted images and unjust systems, negatively affecting the likeness of others and ourselves in God.

Amidst this, another theme that I have seen is the desire to hold onto an identity. Among billions of other people and intricacies of broken systems, people long to be themselves, to be known, and to be autonomous, free. To fulfill this desire, many have gone to lengths of finding new systems and metrics to define who they are. From Myer's Briggs, Enneagrams, to Horoscopes, Branding and other definitions to help understand and realize themselves for who they are. But what is unfortunate about this is how as a result of using these systems, people begin to confine themselves to live the way that they think, but not the unique design that God has made them to be. They are made in the image of God which would entail them to being dynamic containers, ready to receive the fullness of His dynamic love.

In many ways, I have done similarly. I have chosen to let these systems define me as an ENFP-A gemini with 2w3 and 2w1 personality types.[59] I sometimes let these definitions control the way that I treat others and myself even though they are incomplete and unable to fully represent who and what I was designed to be. But honestly, they are good pointers to how I should address the incomplete inclinations of God within myself. But the extent of how some people, including myself, confine themselves to these definitions have become harmful to the faith that we hope to share, the faith that knows no bounds. This faith stretches

---

[59] Myer's Briggs, Horoscope, and Enneagram.

7: COMPLETE IMAGES OF GOD

us, making us malleable containers that are able to respond to love and flex appropriately to the amount that is given.

Maybe I have begun to idolize these structures and as a result have become more rigid and hard-hearted against people who criticize the imperfections of my personality and character. People telling me that I am too spontaneous or never organized would hear me responding with the fact that I am an ENFP, and that there's nothing I or they can do to change that. I have gone so far as to confine myself in these parts of who I am, career, family relationships, church involvement, and friendships. I disregard what people have to say about me, because this is who I am, these are my convictions of who I believe myself to be.

Above is what I believe is a mentality that is harmful to our faith. Instead, the dynamic of the Holy Spirit that has come upon us has made us to be people that are capable of both uniquely changing and appropriately responding. To confine ourselves to metrics that are too rigid would only be a disservice and poor steward of the power that have been given us.

Blurred Lines

But the static construct of society and faith that I've seen most confine and harm people has been the construct of anything sex related. Now in the days of the rising gender and sex revolutions, I find are but only the ramifications of this construct in Christian faith. To clarify, the ways that we have defined gender roles in our Christian faith has been too hurtful and broken.

DYNAMIC: A CHRISTIAN FAITH

DEFINITIONS

But before I go any further, a factor of why many have been unable to address this rise of conflicts lay in their subconscious decision to not set clear lines of what we are working with. So, let me define a few things. There are three things that would help us more clearly see what we need to address.

1. Sex
2. Gender Identity
3. Sexuality

1. SEX

This is the biological definition of what we know humans to be defined by, male or female. Usually defined at birth based off the presence of either male or female genitals and reproductive tissue. Though there is the case of hermaphrodites whom are born with both reproductive systems, partial or complete, as an abnormality found without a normal sex definition.

2. GENDER IDENTITY

This is the gender identity of a person. These are the attributes that we ascribe to male and female people. The makeup of this identity includes characteristics that we define as feminine or masculine. It is something that is also based on cultural context. Each culture ascribe different things to either sex. It is usually something that is found changing due to both nurture and context. But people are found born with certain physical characteristics in which are labeled feminine or masculine as

— 78 —

7: COMPLETE IMAGES OF GOD

well, which can affect the gender identity of the person. Having these characteristics do not define your sex or sexuality, though is affected by sex yet not wholly equated.

3. SEXUALITY

These are preferences that pertain to a person's sexual and romantic attraction. These are also found changing due to nurture, context, and culture but by my definition are also the choices of the individual.[60] These do not define your gender identities or your sex, but are affected by them.

That might have been a lot of ideas to look at but identifying these definitions will help me better communicate what I'm going to talk about.

Fluid Identities

Here's where I start what I've been setting up this entire chapter to talk about. I want to propose an idea of seeing people more dynamically especially through the lens of faith. This stems from the way that we see who God is and how He has made us as well.

> "So God created man in his own image,
> in the image of God he created him;
> male and female he created them."
> (Genesis 1:27 ESV)

---

[60] If something was considered changing in the context of this conversation, it is considered fluid, moving and dynamic you might call it.

DYNAMIC: A CHRISTIAN FAITH

In the Genesis story, God is described as one who has created people, both male and female in His image. But this leads me to the question, "Does that mean that God is both male and female as well?" Throughout the rest of the Bible, we understand that God is a father so it must not be possible that He is both male and female. He is a father to Jesus. So then, "what does this mean of who God is, especially when He uses His image to create both male and female?" I've understood, as I've read more of God in the Bible and through my experiences, that God is capable of loving us both in a fatherly way and a motherly way, looking different depending on the context that you're in. What we usually attribute those characteristics to are masculinity and femininity.[61]

Follow me through the rest of this thought process but don't feel the need to agree. God's image includes both 100% masculinity and 100% femininity, making it possible for Him to create male and female in His own image.[62] Though this does not mean that God is both male and female. But what I reason is that Adam was not created with 100% masculinity or Eve with 100% femininity, but were made with both characteristics. Meaning, Adam and Eve both had some percentage of masculine and feminine characteristics when they formed. I say this because of how even leading up to the fall, these characteristics were apparent. In the garden, right before they sinned, we see Eve take up the more leading role of the relationship, one usually attributed to the masculine partner, the man. Adam also takes the submissive, feminine, role of the relationship in taking the fruit

---

[61] Pulling these gender identities from the American context.

[62] Percentages, for the sake of making things easier to comprehend. Maybe it's actually a little more complicated or dynamic than this.

— 80 —

7: COMPLETE IMAGES OF GOD

while not even arguing the fact that they were against what God had commanded. Somehow, what has occurred is the fact that these two displayed both femininity or masculinity. They were made with both sides of our polarizing gender characteristics. So how does this affect us as people?

I believe that our identities as people were made dynamically by God. People, capable of 100% of their own identity, are composed of varying percentages of masculinity and femininity. For example, I may have a gender identity that is composed of 60% masculinity and 40% femininity. This also includes the fact that my physical body structure is also masculine but feminine-leaning. I would say that my brother, with broader shoulders has been made with more masculine physical traits but could possibly be 45% feminine and 55% masculine. More feminine than me.

But in our faith, the way that we have seen it up until now has been tragically unlike so. It is common to believe that women must be feminine and men, masculine. There is no space for masculinity in a woman or femininity in a man. But now, it is constantly being challenged with the current society where women do well in places of authority and where some men desire to be stay-at-home fathers. This reality is showing us that people are, at the very least, acting different from the ways that it has always been believed. As a result of this hardened outlook on gender identities long lived by our faith, people have been oppressed, unable to fully be what God has created them to be. Instead, we have made for ourselves broken images of how loving others look like by forcing them to be within the confines of what

— 81 —

DYNAMIC: A CHRISTIAN FAITH

we define gender identities to be. Where men must be masculine and women, feminine.

To elaborate more on how our current Christian faith has broken people can be through the examples of what has happened to the gay communities. **IF** you were to look at how people were created more dynamically by their gender identity, it would be simple to understand how some men were more feminine than possibly women. **BUT**, I stand to believe that because we have left no room for this understanding of others, we as a body of Christ have chosen to label them as gays or queers because they did not fit in our understanding of gender. We thought them to be sin, not just sinful. As a result, we have forcibly rendered their identity and rights as people lesser. We silenced their voices and forced them to act the way that we knew, understood, and believed. Now, because we have left them no choice, they have instead chosen to define for themselves who they are and how they supposedly have been made to be. Because of so, we have left room for them to even define their sexuality, gender, and sex to be one, just as we subconsciously believe. If we were to say that their sexuality was wrong, they would now ask if then they were made wrong by God. We would exclaim that it was not by God, but rather, the sin that has entered this world. But even then, what we are denying is them, not just their sin, because we have labeled them sin. In my opinion, the broken ways that we have chosen to understand gender identities, at the least, has left them room to decide for themselves that their sex, gender and sexuality are both malleable and who they were created to be despite the truths that we know of sexuality.

7: COMPLETE IMAGES OF GOD

The polarizing gender identities that our culture holds has caused people, who have had gender identities that included a majority of characteristics attributed to the opposite, to be seen and treated like outcasts. They had to either repress these parts of who they were or persevere through the painful marginalization of their identity. Believing that men should be 100% masculine and women 100% feminine, has thrown out the possibility that God has dynamically made people to behold unique gender identities. As a result, we have forced those with these different identities to blur the lines of sex, gender, and sexuality.

BROKEN MIRRORS

Looking through the Bible, I'd say that these are not just ideas of some new mind or new world, but rather of old. Examples might include people like Jacob. Not only was Jacob considered to have more feminine features, he lived femininely through his mother's favoring as well. Because of the way he was nurtured and born, he lived a life attributed more to what women in society were known living as. I would even argue that stories like of Deborah, Eve, Rebecca, Jael, Rahab, Mary, and many other female figures in the Bible, show a masculine side of theirs through leadership, independence, and power. To also look at all the instances of God holding back miracles, death, powers, or works through the lens of limits, boundaries, or character would help visualize these realities throughout the Bible as well.

But one of the more interesting thoughts that have come through my mind is how we as people, individually have been made as complete images of God. Ones that can reflect all glory to Him, but also reveal Him to many others. This might change the way we see faith in how we treat ourselves and each other. Not that we are God, but instead are both a creation of His and an almost priceless value in existence.

Where do we go from here? I don't know, but I would hope this to be a stepping stone to being less hard-hearted to a realization that our view of both people and God are broken and incomplete.

CHAPTER 8:

REVIVAL

DYNAMIC B.C. STORY

THE HARVEST

REVIVAL! YES. Many of us look forward to the day where we will see the faith of many come alive in Christ! But now, sons and daughters are prophesying, the young are seeing visions, the old are dreaming dreams, all filled with the Spirit of God.[63] The time is now and many of us have seen! The harvest has been plentiful but the workers so few.

REVIVAL THE PROCESS, DYNAMIC THE DESTINATION

Many times has revival been the source of my joy. But every time following each time has ended in a sense of feeling

---

[63] Yes, this is a reference.

lost or defeat. It was weird! The whole theme of revival is not very much about feeling dead, lost or defeat! It's about the coming alive of hopefully the faith of many millions! I'm going to share with you this story of mine where "Revival has become the Process and Dynamic, the Destination" after much wrestling with God about revival.

REVIVAL OF FAITH

I was in between my first and second semester, at a conference of InterVarsity USC, January Jumpstart. Here I felt this overwhelming sensation that God was going to do powerful things. Seeing that there was a gathering of different people from all over the world in some of the most obscure circumstances, I made a declaration that on April 9th of that year, 2016, God was going to do something great. It was only the beginning of the year, but there was a gathering of such faith, as if to foreshadow what was to come. At the end of the conference, we were given the opportunity to share our testimony. I proclaimed God's desire to bring abundant life this year, revival, I called it. Later realizing that April 9th was the 110th anniversary date of the Azusa Revival and the day of Azusa Now, a 2016 revival counterpart by The Call. This realization was so faith filling. I felt as if God was going to do something visibly world changing.

Leading to that day I got to research more about what was happening and how to partner with Azusa Now. Its day came and I remembered I had to go to a training for a missions trip I was committed to. So unfortunately, I missed it. I heard what happened but I came back the following week not seeing or hearing about any significant change on campus or from the surrounding community. Weeks passed and still nothing! GOD?! What happened? Did you not intend to do something great and world changing? I know great things happened that day for The Call, but I did not experience or see it. I felt lost, to think that revival was something to pursue at all, to think that thousands would come to faith instantaneously. To think that evangelism was the most necessary part of the of the gospel. This season ended quickly and summer came for the missions trip that I was going on.

REVIVAL OF JUSTICE

The program was called the Los Angeles Urban Program (LAUP) and the missions trip was into Los Angeles,[64] CA. The purpose of this program was to take us into a deeper view of who God was, as one who desires Justice and Love, more so than sacrifice and offering. The program gave us the opportunity to live it out in the depths of the marginalized communities of urban cities.

During my time there, I discovered the depth of our depravity of who we are as humans, that we are only but blinded people seeded with evil. The oppressed communities from mass incarceration, the people used in cheap labor, the ethnic communities that face racism post slavery, and the independence stripped from the native people of America. The injustice that I

---

[64] I know what you might be thinking, "You aren't even going anywhere."

DYNAMIC: A CHRISTIAN FAITH

saw and the need for God in these areas was evident. It's funny though, up until that point, I have never seen or heard this focus of this part of who God was. One who sought to care for the widowed, the fatherless, and the alien. I mean I've read it, but I've never realized this perspective. I began to know more of God in my heart and not just in my mind. To me, this felt like one of the most monumental moments in my walk of faith, the realization of our God as one who desired justice, mercy and humility.[65]

The truth that we were called to as Christians, to do justice, was beautifully communicated here. I began to see God's heart in the work that was being done and the work that needed to be done. Relocation, Reconciliation, and Redistribution.[66] If all the Christians in this world began to understand this part of who God was and started to love mercy, do justice, and walk humbly with Him, we would be living in a radically different place of faith. As a result, without having to worry about evangelical efforts, people would come to faith through what they would see and at the very least have more conversations about the eternal with Jesus. But again, as I finished my time in mission and shared this with others in faith, I felt lost as to where I was going. To think that Social Justice was the most necessary part of the gospel.

---

[65] Micah 6:8

[66] John Perkins' Three R's in "With Justice for All"

REVIVAL THE PROCESS, DYNAMIC THE DESTINATION

I could continue this again and again in different veins of who God is. Prosperity. Charismatic. Fundamentalism. Etc. I realize now that every time I thought about revival and desired for it, though it was well meaning and good hearted, it was only like a wildfire, without direction. I pursued, but always found myself lost when at the end of it. The passion was there, the vision was there, but it always felt short. I thought that revival was the solution, the end goal. But to think that the journey was the end goal was to only set myself up for disappointment when never arriving at a goal. Revival is the process of coming alive, of awakening, of strengthening. It is not the destination in which we strive towards, but instead is what leads us to its destination, dynamic. To arrive at living, constantly strengthening, and flourishing. Revival leads us to being dynamic. The action to a destination.

WHAT DOES IT MEAN

Instead of focusing our efforts on trying to fulfill the results of dynamic with revivals, we should choose to do them with dynamic as the result. To do so, it'll first require us to consider the possibility of our current idolization of revival. It is the talk of conversations among those who desire to love their neighbors. It is believed to be the way to reach the masses. It is the medium in which leaders encourage laypeople to go. It has become the purpose, when it should be the tool. We must fully put our trust in God, by letting go of control, both in mind and heart, for the

Holy Spirit to lead, who points us to Jesus, the fulfillment of dynamic. It is not to say that revival is wrong or unnecessary. Rather, once we see the destination clearly, we'll have a more guided path, one led by the dynamic of the Holy Spirit through the wildfire strength of revival.

CHAPTER 9:

FAITH, A REFLEX

DYNAMIC B.C. STORY

WHAT DRIVES THIS CHAPTER

In my few short years as a Christian, I've learned to see some of the faith of those around me. Despite the fact that some have been Christian for so long, it has pained me to see that their character is still something that requires a miracle. They pride themselves in having been a follower of Jesus for so many years and I even look up to their adversity and perseverance. But when something out of the norm or uncomfortable comes their way, they are found responding in the most unloving and immature way. These are the same Christians who at the very least either subconsciously hates the LGTBQ+ community, or has their second thoughts about those who are not of their ethnicity or culture, or oppresses their own children as a completely different person when at home than at church. In response to any type of change, away from their will, they are hesitant as a result of their complacency. Along with this, what is common among these people that

I got to converse with is how their faith was something that they have grasped with only their mind. But it is not something that we should solely blame them for. The fact is, we perpetuate the decision to follow Jesus as one that is very much logical. So, it is not evident that this decision must not only occur within their mind, but also within their heart.

Though as I have continued my journey with Christ, I've also had the wonderful blessing of meeting those whose character was full of life within the Church. Their faith was evident not only through their words and wisdom, but also through their actions and state of heart. Despite abnormal circumstances or uncontrollable situations, they still held the mind of the Spirit, of Christ. It was most clear that as I saw greater faith, greater character was there as well. In conclusion, I saw that there was at least a correlation between a person's faith and their character.

THE FATHER OF FAITH

But you're probably thinking, "how does reflexes relate to dynamic and faith?" Worry no more, let me explain and share with you what's going through my mind. Beginning with one of my favorite Bible stories, the story of Abraham and the call to sacrifice his son.

> "After these things God tested Abraham and said to him, 'Abraham!' And he said, 'Here I am.' He said, 'Take your son, your only son Isaac, whom you love, and go to the land of Moriah, and offer him there as a burnt offering on one of the mountains of which I shall tell you.' So Abraham rose

9: FAITH, A REFLEX

*early in the morning, saddled his donkey, and took two of
his young men with him, and his son Isaac. And he cut the
wood for the burnt offering and arose and went to the place
of which God had told him.' (Genesis 22:1-3)*

When I read this, what astonished me was that Abraham
didn't question God. Once he heard God, he acted. It's crazy to
think that the God who decided to give you a child when you
couldn't have one would ask you to give back to Him through
sacrifice. Despite this, Abraham responded quickly with no
hesitation, committed even to the very moment of when his
knife was about to drive into the end of his son's life. Quick and
without hesitation. I mean, you can reason that it wasn't quick,
but to be okay with doing it by so early in the morning, that was
definitely full of faith or foolishness(?).

REACTION

I wanted faith like Abraham. Faith that was almost as quick
as his reaction. If I were to hear or feel God nudge me to do
something, I would want to act immediately, react, no questions
asked. But what does a reaction mean? A reaction is the response
to an event. But for me, I want the connotations to include it
as the jolting response to an event, the immediate thoughts
and actions that happen before you can actually think. Like the
reaction that you would have when you accidentally touch a hot
stove, a reflex. To hear God, to feel Jesus, to be nudged by His
Holy Spirit and respond immediately without thinking. To respond
to His love as one who was created to reflect His goodness.

— 93 —

DYNAMIC: A CHRISTIAN FAITH

REFLEX

Is that possible? Can it be possible to have faith that would be able to discern and respond to God immediately? Yes. To me, that is what I see character as. Character, a reflex of faith. I use this phrase to express the depth at which faith should exist. It is at the level in which your thoughts have not intercepted your immediate actions, it is from where your heart lives. To me, that is character, an embodiment of faith and heart, inside the context of the Christian faith. Well, what does that mean? And why should character be described as a reflex of faith?

CHARACTER

First of all, what is character? I'm not going to try to define something that is so well defined in our society. But what I do want to make clear is that character is the result of what the heart of a person is. Through their actions in every part of their life, their character is shown, not just in a few instances. The fruits of who they have become post-choosing Jesus can be seen through the transcendence of these characteristics throughout their entire being and existence.[67]

> Joy – Peace – Patience – Kindness – Goodness – Faithfulness – Gentleness – Self Control – Love[68]

---

[67] Their life, at church, at home, at work, with their family, with their loved ones.

[68] Galatians 5:22-23

9: FAITH, A REFLEX

LOVE INCLUDES:
Not Envious – Not Prideful – Not Rude – Not Controlling – Not Bothersome – Rejoices with the Truth – Embraceful – Optimistic/Hopeful – Enduring[69]

LOVE ALSO INCLUDES:
Compassion, Mercy, Solidarity[70]

These are the fruits of the Holy Spirit. The fruits of it's labor in the life of one who has received its dynamic, its force of continuous activity, change, and progress. Character represents the magnitude of the maturity of a person's faith through their heart. It can be seen through their Habits, their Personality, their Emotions, and their Relationships.[71] And this is what I try to portray with the phrase 'faith, a reflex'. Faith should exist holistically throughout all of who we are, just like character, shown in various ways through the fruits of the Spirit.

For example, self-control is not something that should just exist in our habits like watching tv, or playing games, or eating luxurious foods, or leisurely traveling, but also in our relationships with friends, family, and co-workers. That may look like setting mutually accepted expectations with one another so that either parties wouldn't expect of the other what they do not agree with. Self-control should also be where emotions are, too. Letting your emotions about freely all the time will not be healthy for either you or anyone around you. Not to say that you must repress your emotions all the time, but self-control over when and how you

---

[69] 1 Corinthians 13:4-7

[70] Luke 10:37

[71] There's probably more categories.

— 95 —

DYNAMIC: A CHRISTIAN FAITH

express them are also important factors. Self-control of your personality might look like understanding that yes you may be a certain way sometimes, like introverted or unorganized, but that doesn't mean you should do that all the time even when you know it would be unloving to you or others. The thought process of taking every single fruit of the Spirit and holistically applying it to your life might look similarly.

Having a reflex-like faith is dynamic. Faith that is constantly active, able to respond differently for every instance that comes their way. For every word that is heard from God, the response is both immediate and appropriate.

DYNAMIC REFLEX

One of the most dynamic reflexes that I've seen in the Bible are the ones of Jesus.[72] For example, the story of feeding the five thousand, a result of a reflex of Jesus. Right before that event occurred, Jesus had sent out His twelve disciples in twos. After their return, immediately knowing their exhaustion, Jesus invited them to join Him in finding rest at a desolate place.

> "The apostles returned to Jesus and told him all that they had done and taught. And he said to them, **'Come away by yourselves to a desolate place and rest a while.'** For many were coming and going, and they had no leisure even to eat. And they went away in the boat to a desolate place by themselves. Now many saw them going and recognized them, and they ran there on foot from all the towns and got there

---

[72] Duhhhhh Enoch. That's obvious.

— 96 —

9: FAITH, A REFLEX

*ahead of them. When he went ashore he saw a great crowd,
and he had compassion on them, because they were like
sheep without a shepherd. And he began to teach them many
things. And when it grew late, his disciples came to him
and said, 'This is a desolate place, and the hour is now late.
Send them away to go into the surrounding countryside and
villages and buy themselves something to eat.'"*
(Mark 6:30-36 ESV)

Jesus and His disciples, tired and ready to find a place to
rest, are met with people who desire more of what they just had.
Teaching, Healing, and Life. Interrupted while on their way to rest,
Jesus responds. But it is from His compassion in which He allows
the interruption. And in this moment, compassion was His reflex.

But even before that, there was another reflex, the reflex of
gentleness. Responding to the return of His disciples, Jesus invites
them to rest. Included in the perfection of who He is are the fruits
of the Spirit. They make up who He is and we see that through His
interactions in every level of His being.

BUILDING FAITH AS A REFLEX

So, where do we start? First a quick review, a **reflex** is a
reflection of the **heart** of a person responding. And those **reflexes**
are seen in the form of **character**. **Heart** and **character** help us see
a person's maturity in **faith** because both represent a part of their
faith. But since we are in the context of **faith**, what we need to
build upon are the remaining, **heart** and **character**.

— 97 —

DYNAMIC: A CHRISTIAN FAITH

Heart and Character

I want to start with "what is the relationship between heart and character?" Heart is the state in which a person's earthly responses come from. Character is the summation of every part of what a person is doing in their earthly life. It is what people use to define a person for what they see. But can there ever exist a discrepancy between the heart and character of a person? Inside the context of faith, I believe that if there is, that person would find themselves burning out all the time from being torn within or from their active sin. We find this exact discrepancy within the pharisees in the Bible.

In response to some pharisees' questioning of His disciples' dishonor of tradition, Jesus shares a parable that targets not only the fallacy of following tradition but also how character and heart work together.

> "Do you not see that whatever goes into the mouth passes into the stomach and is expelled? But what comes out of the mouth proceeds from the heart, and this defiles a person. For out of the heart come evil thoughts, murder, adultery, sexual immorality, theft, false witness, slander. These are what defile a person. But to eat with unwashed hands does not defile anyone." (Matthew 15:17-20 ESV)

Within this explanation, Jesus describes how what comes out of the mouth is what actually defiles a person, not what they take in. But this is merely the most surface level of what Jesus is actually communicating, based off of his previous instructions about the Law at the sermon on the mount.[73] What Jesus implies is that what is of the mind is from the heart. Just as your words are from your mind, so are your actions. As a result, what you do is both a reflection and a direct change upon the heart of a person.

Changing the Heart and Character

So reflexes are from the heart, and that can be seen through character. Though from what you do, say, or think, affects the heart. These actions are the ones that come from a cycle of your thoughts and your heart. So to change your heart would require something of what you do. But if you just do things differently, aren't you similar to what the pharisees were like, where their heart and actions still didn't align? That's true, out of our own efforts we can't change that much. To really change requires a miracle. It requires the power of God. His dynamic, the force that is continually active, changing, and progressing.

You must be thinking, "well then, what difference does this make if I can't do anything out of my own accord?" To answer that, the difference is our approach, our mentality, or some might call our mindset. The difference between now and before is that we are no longer reading the Bible just because we are supposed to, or praying because we should, but because it is the only way we can fully receive God's dynamic to allow for change within our hearts. The change that will help us to desire to love Him and love others more.

---

[73] Matthew 5 - Jesus's extremity here is shown through how He takes the degree of the commandments to a deeper level.

Meditation

Doing something with a different mindset is not an easy feat. It requires that we constantly think about how we are going to respond before we actually get to the point of both doing something different or doing it with a different mentality. If you wanted to be good at anything, whether it be sports, socializing, school, or cooking, you need to first get yourself into the place of constantly thinking that you want to be better at it. Constantly meditating on the different scenarios that you will have to face.

Here's an example. Say you want to be more kind and considerate to the person you're living with. You might get yourself to do it maybe once or twice, then find yourself forgetting that you wanted to be a day or two later. Not only are you frustrated at the person you're living with but also with yourself. So instead, a way you might be able to do it every single day would include thinking about it almost constantly. This might include thinking about how you can be kind or considerate when they don't want to wash the dishes, or decide to leave the lights on at night, or never takes out the trash. Once you start thinking about it every waking moment, while doing it, you'll soon find yourself seamlessly responding as if it were a reflex to any and every situation.

Doing this with God's word and through prayer with Him while trying to do things differently will help build this faith of yours with God. It sounds cliche, but the difference between this and building healthy habits is that the motivation here is not to be healthy or to be good, but to be in a fulfilling and loving relationship with God. The goal is not just to meditate on God's

9: FAITH, A REFLEX

word, but to let it be the medium in which we hold onto the dynamic that God has given us through His Holy Spirit. Not doing so will make it easy for us to lose sight of it and begin to step away from His dynamic. Without the right approach, or mindset, true and faith-filled character will not be formed. There you will find the pharisee within. Just like those whom I've met with their characters in great need of a miracle, so the same will be for those who do not intentionally choose into letting God build their faith into character, a reflex.

CHAPTER 10:

LOVE

DYNAMIC STORY

LOADED

Love. We all have different definitions, perceptions, and ideas of what we know it to be. Some of us know it in the context of romantic relationships. Some in the context of parental or sisterly or brotherly love. Some in the context of best friends, hobbies, or religion. Love, one of the most loaded words in all existence.

WHAT IS LOVE? DON'T HURT ME

Before I get anywhere with what I'm thinking about, I want to clear the air of any connotations that might be attached to the love you know of. The love that I'm going to talk about is not one that is specifically about romance and especially not a sexual one. This is the love that is very much emotional and spiritual yet not designated towards any one thing. Love on its

DYNAMIC: A CHRISTIAN FAITH

own is what I want to take this chapter towards, the type that I see as the love of God.

ONE THING is for sure, I am not so experienced in life that I would have an authority to speak on these things. I just want to imagine the truths of what the implications for love might be in the context of a faith that is dynamic. I'm going to take the idea of how God is love[74] and dynamic,[75] combining them to form how love is also dynamic. I will try my best in hopes that someday, others might take this further.

LOVE AND FEAR

A confusing topic found in the Christian view is the one of fear, fear of the Lord, of God. I know this is a little off-topic but stick with me. Views of fear range from how it is the beginning of wisdom to how it is a reverence or to how through it, God grants blessings. In my short few years as a Christian, I've had the honor of leading some others closer to Christ, many younger than I. An assignment I had one do earlier in our time together was to read through Proverbs, one chapter a day and to journal about it in response. About half-way through, they asked, "What really, is the fear of the Lord? And how does it exist with the perfect love of God that casts out all fears?" -- So quickly did it become confusing in just two books of the Bible![76] Those

---

[74] 1 John 4:8

[75] From Chapter 1.

[76] "Love drives out all fear..." 1 John 4:18

— 104 —

10: LOVE

were powerful questions that I had only thought of seldom. My response was vague yet profound, in my opinion.[77]

> "The fear of the Lord... It's a huge topic. There's a lot that makes up the fear of the Lord. It's not an instance of a thing or an existence of a singular feeling, emotion, or experience. It is an all encompassing truth/knowledge/wisdom that transcends, enters, and is lived out by a person.
>
> The fear of God is not one that is negative, but is rather positive. A fear that means there is nothing else to fear but only of the Lord. Not fear of this world. Not fear of this circumstance. Not fear of the unexpected. Not fear of the future. No fear can equate to the fear of the Lord. Because to equate anything with the fear of the Lord is to equate that with God Himself, to downplay Him, to remove power from Him. To have the fear of the Lord not only includes having a fear of nothing else but also to have His overwhelming and perfect Love. Because His love casts out all other fears, making Him the only fear."

For me, to fear the Lord almost translates to fearing Him through understanding His perfect love. Especially, His love for me. Not to mistaken it as a way to love Him, but to learn how to simply receive His. If this were the truth, it would make understanding Deuteronomy 10:12 more relational as "fearing" is the first in the list of invitations.

> "And now, Israel, what does the LORD your God require of you, but to fear the LORD your God, to walk in all his ways, to love him, to serve the LORD your God with all your heart and with all your soul, and to keep the commandments and

---

[77] (: Heh... heh... heh.

statutes of the LORD, which I am commanding you today
for your good? Behold, to the LORD your God belong heaven
and the heaven of heavens, the earth with all that is in
it. Yet the LORD set his heart in love on your fathers and
chose their offspring after them, you above all peoples, as
you are this day."
(Deut 10:12 ESV)

To fear the LORD your God is about responding through a clearer understanding of God and of His perfect love for you.

THE BASIS

What does this require of us? Outside of viewing faith as dynamic, it might be hard to envision it other than the fact that you need to read more of the Bible to truly know what love is. Maybe you might even want to try to 'feel' more of His love. But most of the time, you're lead towards the idea of understanding more of His grace to 'truly' understand His love. Though there is truth here, it is not what I want to go into.

Inside a dynamic faith, at the center, is our dynamic God, Jesus. By declaration of 1 John 4:8, God is love. As a result, I believe love must also be dynamic, God's love especially. But at the very least this means that love is dunamis.

Love is power. Love is force. Love is might. Love is ability.
Love is efficacy. Love is energy. Love is meaning.

Additionally, dynamic might help us with understanding more of what love might look like. The parts of the definition of dynamic that I want to draw upon love include how it is a force of change, continuous activity, and different according to the situation.

UNEXPECTED AND UNKNOWN

Love is a force of change. When fully understood and received, it should help produce change within us. Change that makes us different. Change that sets us apart. Change that makes us salt. Change that makes us light. It is not the love that we desire, but the love that we need. The one that only God can provide, which inevitably molds us to become more and more like His beloved Son, Jesus.

But this change is not something that always happens in the blink of the eye. It is not a change that happens when you want it. This is the type of change that will always take us into the uncomfortable, the unsafe, the unknown, and the way where there seems to be no blessing. Time and time again, when a person chooses to begin the process of acknowledging the love of the Father, of God, these aspects begin to appear. The continual process manifests in every shape and form. Sometimes, it is leaving everything you've ever known,[78] or running away from an

---

[78] Abraham

DYNAMIC: A CHRISTIAN FAITH

outraged brother,[79] or being sold into slavery by your family,[80] or dying by crucifixion as a criminal.[81]

LOVED BY THE UNSEEN

Just as the results are when the love of God is received, so is how I believe the process it is given, unexpected. The way God chooses to love, is something that I've seen to be different for every other believer I've met. It is not just a simple audible voice or a big miracle. It's very much anything imaginable and more through the character of God. There are unifying characteristics like His constant pursuit or transcendent peace of mind. But more explicitly, it can range from being spoken to by friends, being taken to the depths of this world by strangers, being brought down to your knees by the simplest of things in existence or just being given the world. To expect love to come a certain way especially by one who is unseen is something I believe even children deem foolish. Boxing in the unseen to what is seen is but an idol built by your own mind and doctrine. What comes from the unseen is unexpected, but one thing that I dare to hope is that it will always be good. The type of good that is overwhelming and incomprehensible in every aspect yet made transcendent for our souls to experience deeply. Sometimes it is seen or felt the same but many other times is not and is different. It continues to spark our love-tastebuds and pique our minds with marvelous colors.

---

[79] Jacob

[80] Joseph

[81] Peter

10: LOVE

"LOVED BY THE UNSEEN" – SHOSHANA TAI

Salt and Light, I might call it. His love is constantly like this, perfectly grounding us to Him.

90% OF GOD'S LOVE

But exactly how does God love? I argue that the way God chooses to love people 90% of the time is through other people.[82] Yes, 90% of God's love for you is shown through other people. Leaving people out of your life will make it that much harder for God to love you because if you are not intentional with seeking out His love in the other 10%, you will also miss it. This other 10% of God's love is shown through miracles, works of nature, meditating on His Word, prophecy, prayer, and all the more difficult to experience features of faith. Most of the time, the ones attributed with these experiences of the 10% are usually those that are considered intellectual and further along in their faith. Though this is not necessarily so, I also find that without this 10%, experiencing the perfect love of God would be incomplete.

The most common question that comes as skepticism to this mindset is how ridiculous the percentages are; How could I have the audacity to set such limits on how God chooses to love us? In essence the challenge is, how important are people in the faith that follows Jesus? I want to quickly lay out where I attempt to argue this case.

---

[82] Enoch, you literally built a box right here...

10: LOVE

Over the past few years, one passage that has gotten me to the edge of my seat in curiosity and tension was the great commandment by Jesus.

> "But when the Pharisees heard that he had silenced the Sadducees, they gathered together. And one of them, a lawyer, asked him a question to test him. "Teacher, which is the great commandment in the Law?" And he said to him, "You shall love the Lord your God with all your heart and with all your soul and with all your mind. This is the great and first commandment. And a second is like it: You shall love your neighbor as yourself. On these two commandments depend all the Law and the Prophets." (Matt 22:34-40 ESV)

The interpretation of this text has always placed this irreconcilable battle within my mind. On one hand, people believed that in the second part, Jesus was inviting people to love others as themselves, interpreted as needing to be able to love themselves before loving others, self-love. On the other hand, Jesus invited people to deny themselves[83] while Paul said that one must count others more significant than oneself.[84]

Everytime I reread this commandment, I felt the tension of each side pulling from one to the other. But only recently did I begin to read the second part differently. To better understand what Jesus might have communicated here through this second part would be to complete the sentence as, "... love your neighbor as yourself ..." are already loved. The flow of thought and sentence becomes more fluid as you begin to see it this way. This

---

[83] Matthew 16:24

[84] Philippians 2:3

— 111 —

DYNAMIC: A CHRISTIAN FAITH

"SELF-LOVE" - CATHERINE WU

10: LOVE

way of reading the text brings into unison the side that talks about what Jesus and Paul were inviting us into.

More on the implications of this, self-love does not work in this faith. Self-love is not necessary to love others. It's as if we took those extension cords with extra outlets and took the plug and plugged it into itself to believe that energy will flow. We know this wouldn't work.

This thought didn't come out of nowhere though. In John 13, Jesus explicitly commands His disciples what they must do.

> "A new commandment I give to you, that you love one another: just as I have loved you, you also are to love one another. By this all people will know that you are my disciples, if you have love for one another."
> (John 13:34-35 ESV)

The command is not for us to love one another because we know how we can love ourselves, but the fact that Jesus has already loved us while also loving us now. Following this part of the command, Jesus clearly explains that it is the love that we have for one another that shows that we truly follow Him, not our love for ourselves. We must love our neighbors as ourselves are already loved. Self-love is not necessary, we are already fully loved by God. Though, do not mistaken self-care for self-love for they are two different things.

To drive this home, the use of people in the work of God leads us all the way back to Abraham, the father of this faith. In

DYNAMIC: A CHRISTIAN FAITH

his story, God makes a promise to Abraham, declaring what He will do through him.

> "I will make you into a great nation,
>   and I will bless you;
> I will make your name great,
>   and you will be a blessing.
> I will bless those who bless you,
>   and whoever curses you I will curse;
> and all peoples on earth
>   will be blessed through you."
> (Genesis 12:2-3 ESV)

Very clearly, God declares the first promise and command through Abraham, to bless him that all peoples on earth would be blessed through him and his descendants. Plainly put, people are important to God's work.

LOVE THROUGH THE IMPERFECT

Back to the idea of 90% of God's love, the challenging question comes into play: "How can I experience love through other people when they are so imperfect?" The way that one person chooses to love me may not be the way that I would receive well. For example, I really enjoy intentional time spent with another person, but if the other person only knows how to give gifts while in passing, I would not understand or recognize that love. Each person's list of love languages are unique to them, even the minute details of how those love languages would be most recognizable to them.

10: LOVE

How do we experience the perfect love of God through the imperfect people around us? The challenge is for us to learn how to receive all their different types of love. God is constantly trying to love us through the people around us, but the problem is not that His love is not enough, it is that we do not know how to receive it through all the vessels He uses. If we begin to learn how to see God's love through the attempt of those around us, no matter how imperfect and broken they are, I know that our experience of God's love would begin to overflow into incomprehensible amounts. If you knew how to receive God's love through everyone in your life, you would feel so so loved, whether it be friend or foe. It would be without question that your experience of His love would be so tangible and close.

People are important to the work and love of God. Therefore, the more people you are exposed to, the more opportunities there are for you to receive God's love for you.

EXPERIENCING PERFECT LOVE

What is true of your reception of love is the same of your giving of love. As you meet and get to know more people, the surface area in which you can love God becomes greater. You might ask, how can you love God through people? Jesus puts it simply while replying to those who questioned how they loved Him through their love for people.

> *"And the King will answer them, 'Truly, I say to you, as you did it to one of the least of these my brothers, you did it to me.'"* (Matt 25:40 ESV)

— 115 —

The naked that you clothe, the hungry that you feed, and the stranger that you welcome are all whom Jesus experiences your love through. There are a countless amount of ways of being loved and to love, but we must learn them all that we would be able to receive and experience the fullness of God's love. Because the one thing I believe that is crucial to experiencing the fullness of God's love includes the idea of how love is like a river, living water. Before I continue, let me leave this quote with you to dwell on;

> "To be loved is powerful. But if you let that love stop there it becomes dead. Love is not meant to stop with you. It is meant to be flowed through you. You will experience the deadness of it if you let it stop with you. Instead, love others as you, yourself are loved. Real life and joy is experienced when the love flows through your life, not just into it."

The fullness of God's love for us can be experienced when we not only learn how to receive His love through other people but also are able to let that love pass through us to those around us. The great commandments given to us by Jesus were intentional in that they were meant to help us realize that the flood gates of heaven were not just in the sky, but also as the lives that we carried. To fulfill more of our purpose, we must open and let the living water pass through us. We must go and love God and others for us to truly experience the love that God has for us.

LOVING THE SEEN

But the greater question is the one that addresses how we might go on with loving others. The hope is that we would be

10: LOVE

able to love like Jesus loves. I would hope that we could do so but impossibly, we are imperfect. Nonetheless, we must strive towards doing so. What I am implying for us here still in this existence, is the fact that we must learn to not only receive God's love in different ways, but also love others in different ways. Ways that might take them to the uncomfortable, to the risky, to the counter-cultural. I don't mean the hurtful ones where we push them till they fall off the edge or become traumatized, but just to the doorstep of their comfort zone. Sometimes this takes receiving a cold shoulder for a few moments, but when done gracefully and moderately, not only will your bond with them become a little stronger, but so might their relationship with God be as well as they become more willing to go deeper into the wilderness with Him. Only there would we receive the fullness of God's love.

All of this only comes at the start of receiving His perfect love, fearing the Lord. Dynamic love is what I hope to imagine this. The love of God that is dunamis, full of the force of change, continuous activity, and uniqueness to the person and situation.

CHAPTER 11:

MOMENT BY MOMENT

DYNAMIC B.C. STORY

When were you saved? How were you saved? Why are you saved? For some of us, we won't have the answers to those questions because the forerunners of our faith, our parents, raised us in a faith-conducive environment. So it was not so much a moment, but a process. But for others of us, we would respond without hesitation the specific day of our baptism with the name of Jesus included somewhere in between and that it was by grace through faith.

I like that. There's a beauty to that sort of dedication and honor. It's powerful. But there's one thing I have always been disturbed of by some of those who go out to share the gospel. Their pursuit of having their victim confess with their mouth their sins and that Jesus is Lord, helping them conclude that they are done and now ready after that moment. Now they can be in heaven to be with Jesus for eternity. Yes, it's Biblical but I have seen those of whom have chosen this faith and decide to leave later, yet were they not saved at or after that moment?

Some would argue "no, that their decision was not genuine. What they said was not from the heart." Some would argue "no, it was never intended for them." Others would argue "yes, but because they did not repent, they now are not."

IDOLIZATION & SIMPLIFICATION

We tend to simplify faith down to that moment. Idolizing and simplifying it to the point of setting up people, who are making a decision of faith, for an unrealistic expectation that everything will now be better. Rather, it is now the beginning of the hardest journey of making that same decision every single day, day by day.

We have all been too caught up with trying to determine the future of the lives of everyone spiritually. We have begun to idolize the moment of faith that we invite millions to decide upon. Our desire for instant gratification of our work has led us to perpetuate this faith worldwide that we have become frustrated with the fact that there now exists millions of lukewarm believers. Believers who are content with what they have received or complacent with the easy life of Sunday-going or Sunday-church-serving.

For those of us that know to the exact date of when we were saved, we sometimes alienate those who are trying to step into faith. Making them think that the moment is the only most necessary experience or event to realize salvation by grace. We alienate those who will never experience that moment but are instead journeying through a process. They might be the ones that were born into a Christian family. The ones that were pretty much Christian since they were born. They could also be the ones with no spiritual background. And for many others are those who don't have a complete revelation the first time. But when they continually see the glorification of testimonies of those whom have a Paul-like conversion, it makes them wonder, "where was my moment? Am I really saved then?" Instead, for them, they must make a small decision every single day to follow Jesus. Through honoring their parents, going to school, reading the Bible, not getting drunk. But because they are encouraged to instead have that moment, their hearts struggle with these little decisions. These decisions are now not from their faith, but from their doubt because their experience has been made distant from the "normal" decision of faith.

DAILY BREAD

Many friends, neighbors, and believers I have met have had this reality of their uncomfortable alienation in the faith. One day, early in the morning during my time of devotion, I came across this passage that enlightened the way that I began to think of faith. It challenged the way that I knew it to be for so long. Jesus speaking:

> *And he said to all,* **"If anyone would come after me, let him deny himself and take up his cross daily and follow me. For whoever would save his life will lose it, but whoever loses his life for my sake will save it. For what does it profit a man if he gains the whole world and loses or forfeits himself? For whoever is ashamed of me and of my words, of him will the Son of Man be**

DYNAMIC: A CHRISTIAN FAITH

> *ashamed when he comes in his glory and the glory of*
> *the Father and of the holy angels. But I tell you truly,*
> *there are some standing here who will not taste death*
> *until they see the kingdom of God."* (Luke 9:23-27 ESV)

The word that I want to focus on is the word "daily." Jesus
invites those listening and following Him to deny themselves
and bear their cross **daily**. To me, this implied that you had to
decide to do this **daily**. Everyday, there is an opportunity to deny
yourself and pick up this cross of not saving yourself and instead
the burdens of following Jesus. Yes, following Jesus comes with
burdens. It is not easy, and it never was. Jesus bore His cross
daily knowing that He would have to die. He would have to suffer
one of the most excruciating deaths, cruxification on His cross
bearing all sins of this existence of the world. He invites us to
do the same. But by His grace, this choice is there every day. To
choose into Him. I want to share with you an excerpt from my
journal on reflection of this.

> *"The fight against phone games is hard.[85] It swells when*
> *I'm also struggling to fight the good fight of dying to*
> *myself daily. Now that I think about it, taking that*
> *literally. I think it means that your faith restarts or*
> *begins new each morning. Being Christian is a daily*
> *thing. Anything you've done in the past, even your*
> *confession of faith does not carry over to the next*
> *day. So, Enoch, do you live day by day on and with the*
> *cross? The cross of faith meant to be carried daily by*
> *starting new each morning? Faith is not a moment. It*
> *is a substance to be grasped each day like the manna in*

---

[85] Yes, I was and can possibly still be addicted to phone games. They're so
fun and portable!

— 122 —

11: MOMENT BY MOMENT

the morning where the fog and its haziness provides.[86]
*We must use it for the rest of the day, but how can you
use it if you don't grab it each morning? Daily bread IS
FAITH!"*

We have simplified faith to a moment, a static instance. But
I challenge us to think about faith dynamically. The dynamic of
the Holy Spirit has come upon us. Every day we are changing,
constantly different from the day before. As a result, we must
make the decision to follow Jesus every day to constantly become
a new creation. Stretching this further to every moment in life,
we are becoming different from each experience that is being
added to who we are. Moment by moment we must decide if we
will follow Jesus or not. The moment of when you're driving in
traffic, the moment when that annoying person is talking, the
moment when you're sitting next to people you feel uncomfortable with, the moment of eating breakfast, waking up, or just
breathing. All these moments are times where you must answer,
will you follow Jesus? Will you respond to the altar call, moment
by moment?

If we truly desire to invite the lost into our family of faith,
into this continual battle for this relationship with God, we must
not alienate those who will never experience that moment, but to
instead promote the full breadth of the journeys of faith, moment
by moment.

---

[86] This is a reference to the manna provided to the Israelites by God that
was before dawn where dew would appear. Exodus 16

FINAL CHAPTER:

STATIC

DYNAMIC STORY

Static. Stagnant. Stationary. Still. Inactive. Stubborn. Stuck. Unmoving. Unchanging. Motionless.

If someone were to fit the descriptions above, I would have assumed that they were as good as dead. Lifeless. But the same I would say for a faith that might fit those descriptions, even a god. What do I mean? Dynamic is alive. When we ask about who God is, we need to ask if what we're defining or confining Him to is dynamic or static. Because if we confine Him to something static, we might find ourselves exploring a dead god.

DYNAMIC GOD

One of the characteristics of the Christian faith that set it apart from the rest of the other spiritual faiths is that it interacts with a dynamic God. This God is not one who sits in a heavenly realm never doing anything, rather is one who chooses to relate with His creation. He is the one who chose to come down to this world as a humble servant born in the most now deemed shameful situations. Born to a teenage mother in the middle of an engagement and without a proper place, Jesus was God with us. Not only did he not choose to become a worldly ruler above all nations and peoples, but was instead murdered by His own people as an innocent. In and through Jesus, God interacted with His creation, bringing a redemptive relationship for all to take hold of with him.

STATIC FAITH

But if we view God statically, it can dramatically affect our relationship with Him and with others. The correlation between how we view God and how we live our faith can be that the more static our image of Him is, the more static our faith might be.

How does a static faith differ from the faith that was intended? A static faith is one that believes that there is nothing that needs to be or can be done. It may only be to wait patiently for the end to come. A static faith does not further require anything from the holder, just a single decision. A static faith is one that is formulaic, where something must be done through a specific process. A static faith chooses comfortability and complacency rather than the risky or unknown. Last but not least, a static faith does not require a two-way relationship with God. In fact, it is a man-made religion built to interact with an incomplete, fake, or broken image. God deems this a sin, to make any engraven images of Him, which I might argue is because of how it limits Him. These are the more visible and simple to point out because they are all contrary to the faith and

FINAL CHAPTER: STATIC

gospel that we share as Jesus followers. But the subtle staticity of our faith, more specifically the western one, can be found through simply observing the state of the church today.

WORD FOR WORD

One of the static ways I've seen this faith tend towards is the interpretation of the word of God. Give me just a few more minutes, I'll explain. Word for word people take in sincerity the verses within the Bible. An example of this can be the way I have seen some people idolize the Acts 2 community. To live as a Christian means that you must always sell your belongings and live like those in Acts did. They believe it to be the true depiction of what a Christian community looks like, believing no other way than the first church. While trying to live this out, I believe they miss out on what Jesus has truly intended for them. I'm not saying that the Acts 2 community was not one that we should disregard or not strive towards but rather one that we should learn from to find what that implies for us today. Instead of imitating the literalness of what happened, we should imitate the heart behind it. The heart behind what happened was truly about being both counter-cultural and responsive to the current systems in place, both governmental and religious. Those who began to choose to follow Jesus were outcasts, thrown out from their communities and jobs because of the dominant Jewish and Roman society that they were in.

Rather than to just take the Bible word for word, also allow it to lead us to the heart behind it, God's heart. The hope is not to only memorize the manual to life but also grow into understanding the creator more to creatively live out His intentions for us.

SERVICE AND PASTOR CENTERED

But even now, a large part of the American society has chosen to decide their involvement in church communities based heavily upon services and sermons rather than relationships. Either as a result or as the cause, many churches have begun to stay or become more service and sermon oriented. Maybe this is just a frustration of mine with many christian believers and communities. What is true though is that churches are no longer known as thriving communities where people can grow and mature. Going to church is now known as an ordeal for a day or two a week and for those who want to be good. Relationships have been dissected from christian communities as something to be desired, not foundational. The pressure now lays upon pastors to lead communities solely on presentation, not connection. They are forced to lead the people alone rather than for the people to lead one another together. Maybe that's why some pastors get stressed, burnt, or broken so often. How can they solely move surrounding communities closer to Jesus when the people they're serving are only seeking to be moved by a sermon, not also by fellow brothers and sisters in their own community? Stagnant communities are not solely centered on Jesus, rather are also centered on the structure, pastor, or service that they decide to provide. The service, the pastor have been dynamic, but the hope is that holistically, the entire body would be as well.

FINAL CHAPTER: STATIC

There is always this tendency of ours as humans. When we find something successful, we seek to find a formula or structure that can contain it. Soon after we believe it to be the only way to become successful. This tendency is what I would call being static. There are areas that this would be helpful, say for math, science or technology. But for the christian faith, most of the time, it is not, especially towards God. Dynamic communities choose into embracing Jesus as the center, letting go of the imperfect systems that cannot contain Him and rather upon the relationships that truly embody His love.

THE BEGINNING

You made it to the end! If you find yourself thinking, "This was not as cohesive and comprehensible as he said it would be." You might be right. What I hoped to communicate was not the literalness of my words but rather a heart, a mindset and posture to take in the Christian faith.

To be honest, I could be wrong about everything up to this sentence. I don't believe that I am 100% correct about it all. But, one thing I am sure of is that God is dynamic, not static. He is more than we can ever believe Him to be.

In the following, I share all the other definitions that I see for "dynamic" that I could not fully convey throughout this writing. Writing this, I am ashamed to place the definitions flat out, but I dare not burden you with another hundred pages. They hold the heart of this writing:

DYNAMIC: A CHRISTIAN FAITH

Dynamic is the beautiful unison of creativity and change.

Dynamic is a process-oriented mindset, meaning not just about the end-product, but also the process itself.

Dynamic is spontaneous and improvisational.

Dynamic is both motion and progress, always going forward from one point to the next.

Dynamic is context specific, especially with time, culture, and perspective.

Dynamic cannot be contained and is not a point that is to be reached, rather a state of continuous progress.

Reflecting more on the purposes of this writing, I realized one of them was the desire to take the dichotomies that exist in our faith and break them down to their irreducible roots, to reframe them with a dynamic faith and dynamic God. Some might come back the same, but others might be totally different yet more glorifying to God. Dichotomies can exist, but there are many in our faith that I deem as false dichotomies, ones that don't truly exist but only do because our stubborn and static tendencies have upheld them. My hope is that our definitions, theology, and doctrine would show a God that is alive and near, not one who is dead and distant. I see that our faith is already taking steps towards this as we emphasize our faith as a relationship with God. Relationships are dynamic, right?

Another purpose of this all includes helping myself reconcile the tensions that I held within my heart after reading the Bible in its entirety. I knew that all of it was true, but I felt it calling out to me to understand it more. Dynamic is an attempt to under-standing these tensions that I have held and know should exist.

— 130 —

FINAL CHAPTER: STATIC

In the end, if none of this creates a spark of change within you, my desire is that this would help widen our vocabulary to not only increase our knowing and relationship with Him but also to better communicate this gospel to others.

Throughout this process, I've learned that in the presence of complacency and comfortability, it is not the inability to see the truth that holds us back, but our lack of desiring more of Jesus, more of God, more of His Spirit. What we desire is too little. As a follower of Jesus desiring to live out the gospel, I don't want people to just know Jesus. *It is not enough.* Yes, not enough. I want people to desire Jesus, to thirst for Him. If anything, to want Him more than anything this world can offer. To then continually experience Him, eternally and wonderfully, fill the insatiable dark void within. Maybe that's part of what He means for us to be salt and light. All honor and glory to Him, Jesus Christ!

ACKNOWLEDGMENTS:

I want to thank everyone who has been part of my life. Whether I got to know you personally or not, your part has contributed to who I have become. I could have not been more grateful for your life as a blessing.

More specifically, I want to thank my family and friends who were able to bear the treacherous walk of me being involved in their daily life.

I also want to thank my good friend Mike Parkyn who has been such a brother, encourager, and guide. Without him, none of these thoughts would have come alive to become this writing. I thank God for the heart that has been given him. His heart catalyzes life into those around him.

My thanks to Jim Taylor, a great mentor of faith and fatherhood to me. Blessed were our weekly times together in fellowship and communion with Jesus. His willingness to both listen and teach in response to my life and my heart was more than I could ever ask.

To Hannah Hiler, my beloved friend and sister. She has helped me through the process as well in bringing my life as a Christian into beauty. Designing everything from the margins to the covers, surely God has blessed this world with her life.

Last but not least, to the Spirit who has led me here. I thank God, Jesus, and Him, for their work in and through me. He has been so good to me.